Witchcraft, Sorcery and the Inquisition

ABOUT THE AUTHOR

Carmel Cassar M.Phil (Cantab), Ph.D. (Cantab) is a Fellow of the Cambridge Commonwealth Society, a member of the Royal Anthropological Institute, and a lecturer in history and anthropology at the University of Malta. He is in charge of ethnography with the Museums Department and is mainly involved in the rehabilitation of the Inquisitor's Palace as a Museum on the Anthropology of Religion.

Dr Cassar is the author of a number of studies on Maltese cultural and ethno-history. Amongst his publications one can mention 'Everyday life in Malta in the Nineteenth and Twentieth Centuries' in V. Mallia-Milanes (ed.) *The British Colonial Experience 1800-1964: The Impact on Maltese Society*, Mireva Publications, (1988); 'Popular Perceptions and Values in Hospitaller Malta', in V. Mallia-Milanes (ed.) *Hospitaller Malta 1530-1798: Studies on Early Modern Malta and the Order of St John of Jerusalem*, Mireva Publications, (1993); 'Witchcraft Beliefs and Social Control in Seventeenth-Century Malta', (1993); *Fenkata: An Emblem of Maltese Peasant Resistance*, Ministry for Youth and the Arts, (1994); '*U Mulu di Malta*' The Maltese Trade in Donkeys and Mules', in H. Frendo (ed.) *Storja '96*, University History Society Publication, (1996) and others.

Witchcraft, Sorcery and the Inquisition

A Study of Cultural Values in Early Modern Malta

Carmel Cassar

Mireva
Publication

This edition first published in 1996
by Mireva Publications
of Tower Street, Msida, Malta, MSD 06.
(Mireva and logo are registered trade marks. Reg. no. 17998)
Phototypeset and electronically paged on
MirevaNewCentury SchoolBook 10/12pt by MirevaSet.
Produced by Evan Cumbo.
Printed by Gutenberg Press,
Gudja Road,
Tarxien, Malta.

International Standard Book Number

1-870579-47-X

© *Witchcraft, Sorcery and the Inquisition: A Study of Cultural
Values in Early Modern Malta* — Carmel Cassar — Mireva
Publications (1996)

For
my son
Marc'Andrea

Even before the Reformation, theologians tended to believe in setting limits to kingly power. This was part of the battle between the Church and the State which raged throughout Europe during most of the Middle Ages. In this battle, the State depended upon armed force, the Church upon cleverness and sanctity. As long as the Church had both these merits, it won; when it came to have cleverness only, it lost.

Bertrand Russell, *History of Western Philosophy*, ch.xiv

Galileo, as everyone knows, was condemned by the Inquisition, first privately in 1616, and then publicly in 1633, on which latter occasion he recanted, and promised never again to maintain that the earth rotates or revolves. The Inquisition was successful in putting an end to science in Italy, which did not revive there for centuries. But it failed to prevent men of science from adopting the heliocentric theory, and did considerable damage to the Church by its stupidity. Fortunately there were Protestant countries, where the clergy, however anxious to do harm to science, were unable to gain control of the State.

Bertrand Russell, *History of Western Philosophy*, ch.vi

Contents

Illustrations

PLATES

Abbreviations

ACM	Archives of the Cathedral, Mdina
AIM	Archives of the Inquisition, Malta
AOM	Archives of the Order of St. John, Malta
Civ	Civil Proceedings
Corr	Correspondence
Crim	Criminal Proceedings
fol./s.	folio/s
Misc.	Miscellanea
Ms.	Manuscript
NLM	National Library of Malta
Proc	Proceedings
Vol.	Volume

Preface

The study of the Malta Inquisition tribunal is of relatively recent development. Until the early 1960s interest was mostly directed towards the
Inquisitor's role as an Apostolic Visitor. The opening of the archives to
researchers in 1968 has created an unprecedented interest in the
Inquisition as a tribunal that was particularly concerned with the control
of heretical behaviour on the part of Roman Catholics in Malta and to
check other Christian and non-Christian denominations.

Analytical studies have further shown that inquisitorial documentation may serve as the primary source for the study of matters not directly
connected with the history of the institution. Witchcraft, popular beliefs,
and even the way of life of other ethnically different communities can be
better understood by studying the records of the Inquisition.

In the last twenty-five years, a new generation of historians has
entered the field, with the result that certain preconceived positions –
which caused sterile polemics among critics and apologists of the institution – have now been largely abandoned. The new development has led
to a different approach, previously ignored, which enabled scholars to
broaden their methodology and themes of interest. This situation became
possible since historians of early modern Europe and the Mediterranean
have become aware that they can learn a great deal from social theory
and anthropology. Indeed anthropological theory enabled them, not only
to understand the society which they study, but even to appreciate the
social function of language, myths, emblems and rituals.

The present study is, of course, influenced by this 'new kind of history'
particularly since I am convinced that in the history of perceptions, the
distinction between history and anthropology is often blurred. The
present analysis is restricted to a few basic case-studies at the turn of the
seventeenth century when the witch craze was raging throughout
Europe. In Malta, as in the case of the Italian peninsula, the Inquisitors

– who retained jurisdiction over witchcraft cases – were far milder than the secular judges of continental Europe. Many suspects were either released or else condemned to relatively minor punishments. The Italian inquisitors seemed reluctant to define 'superstitious' activities as sorcery. Finally, the data studied here shows that knowledge of witchcraft was not only widespread, but oral traditions interacted with élite culture.

Over the years in which I have been involved with the Malta Inquisition Tribunal – both as a research assistant and as researcher – I have received help and advice from many people. In particular I should like to thank my Cambridge professors, particularly Peter Burke, Alan Macfarlane and Gilbert Lewis who enabled me to gain invaluable insights into popular culture and values, witchcraft, religious beliefs and popular healing.

For improvements on the penultimate version I am most grateful to Dominic Cutajar, and to Manwel Mifsud who translated and commented on the invocations in old Maltese verse. Biagio Vella has kindly checked and improved the Latin translations in the appendices. I also learned a good deal from discussions with Canon J. Azzopardi and Fr A. Bonnici. A word of thanks goes to the staff of the Cathedral Museum, especially Mr Noel D'Anastas. Prof. Victor Mallia-Milanes gave me the opportunity to prepare a course on popular religious beliefs to BA (Hons) history students. Discussions with the students taking the course did a great deal to clarify my ideas. A special word of thanks goes to those students who have decided to deepen their knowledge of the Inquisition Tribunal and its impact on Maltese society particularly Noel Buttigieg, Tony Camenzuli, James Debono, Ray Debono, Kenneth Gambin and Godwin Xuereb. To them all, and especially to my wife Susan, I owe a debt of gratitude for their moral support.

It is hoped that this study may serve to encourage further research in the history of cultural values and beliefs.

Carmel Cassar
University of Malta
December 1996

Introduction

The Tribunal of the Inquisition in Malta

In popular imagination, the term inquisition is synonymous with terror, torture and repression. Yet the inquisition was a more complex and fascinating phenomenon than any fiction story might suggest. The incredible richness and diversity of inquisition sources make it possible to use its records to shed light on virtually every aspect of social, religious, legal and cultural history.

There were three separate inquisition tribunals: the Medieval, the Spanish and the Roman. In Malta we are mainly interested in the Roman Inquisition which was established by Pope Paul III through the issue of the Bull *Licet ab initio* in July 1542, creating a totally reformed Inquisition, inspired by the recent successes of the Spanish Inquisition. The new tribunal, more commonly referred to as the Holy Office, was mainly intended to oppose the doctrines of Martin Luther and other emerging Protestant groups that were then considered a major threat to the Catholic Church. The Holy Supreme Congregation under Cardinal Carafa (later Pope Paul IV) gained among its many privileges that of appointing inquisitors and the appropriate staff to help each inquisitor in any town or province. There was even an attempt to create an 'Index of prohibited books', including those books deemed likely to propagate 'false teachings'.[1]

---

[1] C. Cassar, 'An Index of the Inquisition: 1546-1575', p.157.

Before the arrival of the Hospitaller Order of St. John in 1530, there already existed a Tribunal of the old medieval Inquisition in Malta. This tribunal was under the jurisdiction of the Bishop of Palermo, and was no different from that of any other Sicilian town. When the Bull *Licet ab initio* was published, Malta had been under the Order's rule for only twelve years. A few months later, Domenico Cubelles was elected bishop, a position he held until his demise in 1566.[2]

The bishopric of Cubelles can be divided into two periods: 1542-1561 when he functioned as Bishop of Malta; 1562-1566 when he also carried out the duties of inquisitor for the Maltese islands.[3] But the Tribunal took another eight years before it was established as a completely separate entity from the bishopric. This came about almost by accident. The reigning Grand Master La Cassiere (1572-1581) sought the Vatican's advice over a quarrel that had ensued between him and Bishop Royas. Mgr. Pietro Dusina, a native of Brescia in Italy, was sent to Malta to acquaint himself with the difficulties between the two most prominent dignitaries of Malta, and to act both as Apostolic Visitor and Inquisitor.

Dusina was granted the faculty to proceed in all cases dealing with the faith, and although his term of office lasted a mere nine months, he managed to augment the authority of the Holy Office. The efficiency of the Holy Office was further enhanced by the short term of office enjoyed by all the inquisitors that came after Dusina.[4]

Established as a separate tribunal from the Bishop's court, the Holy Office could act as a watchdog against all kinds of heretical practices and beliefs. To combat such problems, sixteenth and seventeenth century church authorities undertook broadly conceived programmes of cathecetical instruction for the laity, training for the clergy, and prosecution against religious as well as moral offences in church courts. In post-Catholic Reformation

---

[2] Ibid.

[3] Ibid., pp.158-59.

[4] C. Cassar, 'The first decades of the Inquisition: 1546-1581', pp.207-208.

Malta, as in Italy, the local offices of the Roman Inquisition undertook a systematic campaign to suppress popular errors of belief.[5] Although these categories could shift over a period of time – what was proposed or tolerated in the 1600s could be proscribed two centuries later, or vice versa – they leave one with an impression that there was constant tension between the ruling and subordinate classes, the centre and the periphery. This, very often, brought about changes and compromises on both sides.

The Inquisition enjoyed jurisdiction over everyone. Individuals could either be denounced or made to appear before the Inquisitor admitting guilt. The most common forms of prosecuted practices were heretical behaviour, blasphemy, apostasy, and popular religious beliefs, often referred by the inquisitors themselves as 'superstition'. Yet there was a distinct difference in emphasis throughout the 237 years of its existence. In the initial stages, the tribunal was mostly concerned with heretical behaviour and the reading of prohibited literature due to fear of Protestant influence. In the early seventeenth century, the Inquisition became particularly concerned with the impact left on the ordinary Maltese, especially women, by the ever growing community of Muslim slaves. At that time, the tribunal exercised tight control on popular magical practices. By the eighteenth century blasphemy, marital infidelity and apostasy seem to have been the main worries of the tribunal. One must point out that during the eighteenth century the influence of Inquisition was in decline and its irrelevance becoming increasingly felt. Yet the Maltese tribunal seems to have served as an ideal stepping stone to career advancement for the prelates manning the tribunal. This may explain why twenty four out of sixty three Inquisitors of Malta became cardinals and two of them were elected Popes. Fabio Chigi was elected as Alexander VII and Antonio Pignatelli as Innocent XII.[6]

---

[5] Ibid., pp.207-208.

[6] A. Bonnici, *Storja ta' l-Inkiżizzjoni*, vol. I, pp.275-78, 308 and vols.II (1992) and III (1994) passim.

The Inquisition felt the need to establish itself in the newly urbanised area of Malta where, due to the cosmopolitan atmosphere created by the presence of the Hospitaller Order, people were more liable to transgress against the teachings of the Roman Catholic Church. This may perhaps be the reason why Mgr. Dusina agreed to transform the old Law Courts of the Order's government at Vittoriosa into an Inquisitor's Palace. Probably the officials of the tribunal were in a better position to check and control any unorthodox behaviour in the cosmopolitan Harbour area. It may also explain why the Vittoriosa palace continued to serve as the seat of the Inquisition Tribunal in Malta right up to the time of the French occupation in June 1798.[7] Throughout the rule of the Order of St John, the Inquisitor and Apostolic Visitor could wield great power as the direct representative of the Holy See. This situation enabled the Roman Catholic Church to exert a degree of preponderant influence on all sectors of Maltese society.

Popular Piety

Recent historical studies on sixteenth and seventeenth century Europe have documented a 'reform of popular culture', which P. Burke has described as the religiously motivated efforts of the educated to change the belief and behaviour of the rest of the population.[8] The key concept is reform, in particular as a process that reveals the innate tensions between different levels of society. This can only be accomplished by widening the area of research to a larger time-span than historians are used to.

'Popular religion' and its role in socio-religious studies play a primary role in the study of popular values. In reality, popular religion has relatively little to do with class, because devotions and forms of piety associated with it were shared by the entire population, lay and clerical, literate and illiterate. However, according to

---

7 Ibid., vol. III, pp.531-36; C. Cassar, '1564-1696: The Inquisition Index of Knights Hospitallers of the Order of St John', pp.157-58.

8 P. Burke, *Popular Culture in Early Modern Europe*, ch. 9.

G. De Rosa, there existed a difference in approach towards the phenomenon. The peasants, with a section of the lower clergy, believed in magical beliefs which were partly pagan and partly Christian in origin. Thanks to the intervention of the Roman Inquisition, the Catholic Reformation Church tried everything possible to introduce new forms of Catholic piety based on the principles propounded by the Council of Trent.[9]

Although the focus of modern historiography on most recent research has been on Christianization and popular piety within a context of ecclesiastical history, there has also been a gradual shift from the traditional emphasis on institutions to people and to their actual practices. Therefore in the study of Church history, we see a movement away from official, institutional 'ecclesiastical history', to a broader history of 'religion' or 'piety'; away from theology in the precise, technical sense, towards the study of attitudes, values and sentiments; away from the concerns of the clergy, towards those of the lay majority.[10] It is not a coincidence that a similar shift is observable in the literature and art of the time, better known to us as 'Baroque culture'.

Indeed traditional historians often descibed as 'popular religion' those aspects of the ritual which the ecclesiastical authorities sought to disqualify by using the derogatory term 'superstition'. Yet it is absurd to postulate a 'popular religion' perpetually opposed to that of the Church hierarchy, and to recognise it only in the presence of beliefs, cults and practices deviating from orthodoxy.[11] C. Ginzburg consequently suggests returning religious practices to their wider context of *culture folklorique*, singling out the specific social categories and cultural contacts to which we refer.[12]

In this shift towards an unofficial history of the Catholic Reformation, the French contribution has been of prime importance. It goes back at least to Lucien Febvre, co-founder of the

---

[9] G. De Rosa, *Chiesa e Religione Popolare nel Mezzogiorno*, p.6.

[10] J. Delumeau, *Catholicism Between Luther and Voltaire*.

[11] P. Burke, 'Popular piety', p.115.

[12] C. Ginzburg, 'Stregoneria, magia e superstizione in Europa fra medioevo ed età moderna', pp.119-33; Jean-Claude Schmitt, '"Religion populaire" et culture folklorique', pp.941-53.

journal *Annales*. Febvre burst through the frontiers between disci-
plines, so that he is difficult to classify as either an anthropologist,
a sociologist or a historian.[13] P. Burke opines that

> the new emphasis on the history of popular piety has brought new prob-
> lems in its wake. In the first place, there is the problem of what counts as
> 'popular'... Are we talking about the religion of the laity, including the
> learned, or about that of 'ordinary people', that is the 'subordinate classes',
> the peasants or the illiterate? Or are we talking about unofficial practices,
> whoever was involved in them?

After disputes over definitions and problems of method, how can we
know what the 'inarticulate' masses thought or felt about their religion? If we use popular religious literature, for example, we run the
risk of ignoring the illiterate and also of confusing what was
produced for the people with what was produced by them.[14] Luckily
we do get this type of information from the Inquisition archives,
since the Inquisition transcribed the answers of those accused and
the witnesses (including their gestures); but we have always to be
on our guard against leading questions and also to the fact that the
Inquisition interrogated only a minority. Nonetheless historians
should be well advised not to attempt to isolate the 'people' as an
object of study, but to focus on the interaction between clergy and
laity, rulers and ruled, the highly educated and the more or less
illiterate masses.[15]

Types of Transgression

Errors of belief, characteristic of the transgressors, were summed
up in the recurrent phrase 'ignorance and superstition'. Although
the definition of each of these terms varied along confessional lines,
'ignorance' usually referred to lack of basic doctrinal information,
and 'superstition' always encompassed magical beliefs and practices of the time. Religious complaints about behaviour focused

---

[13] L. Febvre, *The Problem of Unbelief in the Sixteenth Century: The Religion of Rabelais*; P.
   Burke (ed.), *A New Kind of History: From the Writings of Febvre*, pp.xii-xiii.

[14] P. Burke, 'Popular piety', p.115.

[15] Ibid., p.127.

most of all on blasphemy and prohibited sexual behaviour. Official Church quarters often complain about a lamentable state of ignorance, superstition and immorality which was characteristic of the people of Catholic Europe. In Malta these practices were mostly imputed to the activity of Muslim slaves who exerted direct influence on the weaker members of society identified by the Inquisitor, later Cardinal, Federico Borromeo (1653-1655) as mostly women and 'simpletons'.[16] According to B.P. Levack, 'these superstitious people were to be prosecuted of course, but the purpose was to correct and purify the faith, not to protect society from a conspiratoral menace'.[17]

Practices, that the Church condemned, usually had a different meaning for the participants from the one interpreted or perceived by the clergy. This sometimes resulted in a form of cultural disintegration or 'deculturation'. When it involved a dominant and receiving culture, the process was invariably one of acculturation. In the case of Malta, we can adopt a terminology originally earmarked for early modern Italy. Here the term 'negotiation' might be more apt, since it implies a separation and distinction between cultures, without making the gulf too vast, which would render dialogue impossible.[18]

The usefulness of the term 'negotiation' lies in taking account of the active role of the subordinate classes of society in creating their own patterns of behaviour and ritual expression. This is the case with popular healing rituals and the formation of local shrines, often developing into centres for pilgrimage. Popular culture can therefore account for positions of relative weakness, or as A. Prosperi points out, religion is transformed into a force of control, thus maintaining the *status quo* and restraint where the common folk are encouraged not to stray from their own condition – a limit which was not only cultural but also increasingly social.[19]

---

[16] NLM Libr. 23, p.258; 'Relazione di Malta e suo Inquisitoriato: dell'Inquisitore Federico Borromeo', p.189.

[17] B.P. Levack, *The Witch-hunt in Early Modern Europe*, p.201.

[18] P. Burke, 'A question of acculturation?', pp.197-204.

[19] A. Prosperi, 'Intellettuali e chiesa all'inizio dell'età moderna', pp.159-252.

Diabolical Magic

Trials for 'magic and superstition' – acts which the Church believed derived their potency from a tacit or expressed pact with Satan – can tell us much about lay forms of ritual healing, popular and learned magic, as well as diabolical witchcraft. With the help of other sources, we can reconstruct the social, behavioural and ritual contexts in which these operated. There has been a tendency to dwell on the distinction between magical and religious rituals according to the way they were supposed to work: that is, whether a given act had a mechanical efficacy (considered magical), or relied on the intervention of the divine (religious). However, given that so-called magical invocations often gained their efficacy through recourse to saints, and that many religious rituals and devotions were assumed to have automatic effectiveness, it is difficult to maintain this distinction.[20] They are still useful as descriptive terms, although not as categories, and rather than attempt such distinctions, I would prefer to regard healing rituals as part of a wider cultural complex, overlapping with official Church rules and official medicine.

The Roman and Spanish Inquisitions took the diabolical element in popular magic much less seriously than related campaigns elsewhere in Europe. The root cause of what the tribunals labelled 'superstition' was ignorance, and not satanically inspired evil. M. O'Neil's article on the Inquisition's attitude towards love magic is a good example of what can be done with the trial records to shed light on the invocations and conjurations better known as *scongiuri* and *orazioni*. These formed a crucial part of rituals of healing and ceremonial magic and, more significantly, attempt to single out the circumstances under which people were prepared to approach or

---

[20] Recent contributions to the history of popular traditions have revealed much about the social context and workings of ritual healing and its relationships to beneficient and maleficient magic. The following are a few titles referring to studies based in Italy: cf. E. de Martino, *Sud e Magia*; A. di Nola, *Gli Aspetti Magico-religiosi di una Cultura Subalterna Italiana*; A. Rivera, *Il Mago, il Santo, la Morte, la Festa: Forme Religiose nella Cultura Popolare*; T. Seppilli (ed.) *Le Tradizioni Popolari in Italia: Medicina e Magia*.

accuse a cunning man or woman.[21] Nonetheless we must keep in mind that denouncement to the Holy Office does not necessarily equal an actual occurrence, even though the actual accusation may be just as revealing of its social fabric and tensions.

This theme is brought forward in the analytical case study on the military engineer and lay member of the Order of St John, Fra Vittorio Cassar, discussed below. Despite the fact that the study is largely based on a single individual, it suggests that there existed close links between popular and learned (or élite) magic at the local level. The former was often practiced by females and Muslim slaves, while the practitioners of learned magic were mostly clerics, members of the knightly Order, and the professional classes.[22] Learned magic represented by far the greater threat, as far as the Counter-Reformation Church was concerned, despite – or because of – the number of clerics and members of the Hospitaller Order involved in it. Not only did it have a more clearly expressed cosmology than popular magic, but the powers obtained through demons set it out as a rival to orthodox Catholicism.

The Tribunal also tried women for the specific crime of diabolical witchcraft, alleged to result from an 'expressed' pact with the devil and accompanied by night flight to the sabbath gathering. Here, as the case study on Betta Caloiro suggests, one needs to separate demonological myth from the actual practice of witchcraft, and determine its relationship to other popular beliefs particularly where it overlaps with official religion.

Like the Spanish Inquisition, the Holy Office tended to treat female witches as stupid and misguided.[23] This went hand in hand with the Inquisition's concern for procedural propriety, the rare use of torture, and assigning little weight to the denunciations by previously accused witches.[24] The Inquisition's relative leniency in such

---

[21] M. O'Neil, 'Magical healing, love magic and the Inquisition in late sixteenth-century Modena', pp.88-114.

[22] C. Cassar 'Witchcraft beliefs and social control in seventeenth century Malta', pp.324-27.

[23] W. Monter, 'Women and the Italian Inquisitions', p.85.

[24] J. Tedeschi, 'Inquisitorial law and the witch', pp.83-118.

instances was combined with a war on 'superstitious healing' during the late sixteenth and the first few decades of the seventeenth centuries, as pointed out in a wide ranging study on several Italian tribunals by G. Romeo.[25] Although probably not a conscious strategy, this 'witchcraze' helped to diffuse the perceived threat of witchcraft. Still magical activities were considered to be the reverse side of sorcery or *maleficium* (accusations of which culminated in the witch-craze in many areas of northern Europe). Romeo also seeks to demonstrate the extent that exorcism developed during the same period. Because exorcism could be employed against both suspected witch and the victim, in order to chase away demonic influences, it served as a further escape valve for perceived witchcraft threats. All of this fits in the context of increasing Church control that the author terms 'clericalization' after the enforcement of the principles of Trent.[26] Due to the fact that the Holy Office was part and parcel of the post-Tridentine system, it could assert its authority over all 'religious offences', appointing its own inquisitors (rather than depending on Dominican and Franciscan friars as in the past), and through whom it was able to exercise direct control.[27]

There is still much to be learned about witchcraft at the local level, especially if we analyse the trials and accusations from both 'above' and 'below'.[28] The historiography of witchcraft studies has until now been strongly influenced by anthropological functionalism and thus not really interested in the symbolic dimension of beliefs. In other words, it fails to answer the delicate issue: How were people's beliefs influenced by trial procedures? A useful example is found in C. Ginzburg's study of the *benandanti*, a Friulian cult, whose members 'went out' at night to do battle with witches in order to defend the harvest.[29] Ginzburg demonstrates

---

[25] G. Romeo, *Inquisitori, Esorcisti e Streghe nell'Italia della Controriforma*.

[26] Ibid.

[27] C. Cassar, 'The first decades of the Inquisition: 1546-1581'.

[28] P. Burke, *The Historical Anthropology of Early Modern Italy*, pp.79-80.

[29] C. Ginzburg, *The Night Battles: Witchcraft and Agrarian Cults in the Sixteenth and Seventeenth Centuries*.

how the beliefs of the *benandanti* were transformed over the course of several centuries through interaction with inquisitorial judges into those of standardized diabolical witchcraft, leaving only vague traces of earlier beliefs. This process of diabolization also occurred in Sicily. In an illuminating study on a Sicilian fairy cult, G. Henningsen shows how the *donni di fuora*, were reputedly organized into companies that went about visiting houses at night to heal people and bestow prosperity. Interestingly enough, soon after 1600, the accounts of the ritual celebrations of these *donni* were turned into straightforward witchcraft accounts as a result of the Inquisitors' 'monkish fantasies'.[30] Such cases lend some credit to the 'amateurish and absurd' view, originally put forward by M. Murray, as to the survival pre-Christian fertility cult.[31]

The general trend taken by witch hunts in early modern Malta, as in the rest of Europe, was essentially an attack on defenceless members of society, who at most times were considered a threat to the established system, simply because they did not conform.[32] This explains why, during the first quarter of the seventeenth century, relatively large numbers of women, mostly from the urbanized Harbour area, were accused *en masse* of witchcraft activities. Why did people look at the Inquisition for protection from wise women and Muslim slaves rather than turn to traditional remedies against their activities? It may have been due to changing socio-economic conditions, since structures were changing fast at the time. But it was also because in part this suited the people's own needs, who thus found scape-goats to put under accusation;[33] partly

---

[30] G. Henningsen, '"The ladies from outside": an archaic pattern of the witches's sabbath', pp.191-215.

[31] M. Murray, *The Witch-cult in Western Europe*, p.12.

[32] C. Cassar 'Witchcraft beliefs and social control', p.329.

[33] Prostitutes plied their trade in the service of knights and other members of the Hospitaller Order, as well as for tradesmen, sailors, soldiers and men of fortune. At the same time the ever growing presence of male Muslim slaves who were most often adherent to a rival religion, and who furthermore comprised a sizeable minority, helped to generate unethical behaviour among the inhabitants. C. Cassar, 'Witchcraft beliefs and social control', passim; A. Bonnici, *Il-Maltin u l-Inkiżizzjoni f'Nofs is-Seklu Sbatax*, Malta, 1977, ch.2; Ibid., *Storja ta' l-Inkiżizzjoni*. vols I & II.

also because the Church stressed that such sorcery was the devil's work, since only the Church possessed the force and authority to counter it. As R. Horsely points out, a witchcraft accusation was all the more plausible against someone who already had a reputation of a wise woman.[34] Nonetheless, the vast majority of trials initiated as charges of specific malefice, believed to lie behind particular diseases or misfortunes, rather than as charges of diabolical witchcraft. Wise women and Muslim slaves were tolerated as a necessary evil – on the principle that 'whoever knows how to cure, knows how to harm' (*qui scit sanare, scit destruere*).[35]

A non-conforming attitude in a highly conformist society, led to harassment from all sides, and all such individuals became prone to similar accusations.[36] Thus 'prostitutes' and Muslim slaves were the two sectors of society most liable to charges, that explains why A.R. Cardozo was able to remark upon the social, political and religious intolerance that provide the initial impetus for a craze.[37]

What do the inquisitorial records contribute to the study of supernatural remedies in early modern Malta? The existence of parallel and competing remedies to the problems of everyday life is one indication of the tensions between cultural levels at the time. The identity of purpose and the structural similarities shared by 'orthodox' and 'popular' remedies indicate that these alternatives existed within the same system. It may thus be helpful to view religion as a ritual system made up of individual 'signs' or 'symbols',[38] which offer various means of gaining access to sacred power so as to provide protection and maintain personal equilibrium.

---

[34] R. Horsely, 'Who were the witches? The social roles of the accused in the European witch-trials', pp.689-715.

[35] P. Burke, *Popular Culture in Early Modern Europe*, p.107.

[36] C. Cassar, 'Witchcraft beliefs and social control', p.329.

[37] A.R. Cardozo, 'A modern American witch-craze', p.469.

[38] C. Geertz, *Interpretation of Cultures*, pp. 87-125.

Witchcraft and Sorcery

Inquisitorial Procedures in Magic Accusations

In recent years historians have devoted much effort to the phenomenon of witchcraft, and though some very expert work – largely
influenced by anthropological studies[1] – has been carried out, there
seems to be no clear notion about the meaning of the term 'witchcraft'. Here we will try to explore the phenomenon both in terms of
the inquisitorial procedures employed and with regards to its
meaning and place in popular beliefs and practices of the times
under study.

Since the activity of the Inquisition tribunal was influenced by
the works of demonologists, many of whom wrote from their past
experiences as inquisitors, their ideas too may be relevant to the
analysis.

Confessors did their utmost to convince people that the best way
of reacting against acts of suspected sorcery and witchcraft was to
resort to the Inquisition tribunal. Such circumstances explain why
denunciations and confessions alike frequently began by citing the
confessor's suggestion to bring the case to court; indeed absolution
often depended on it. Thus when Dominica de Candia of Għaxaq
was in peril of miscarrying her baby, several women suggested that

---

[1] See for example A. Macfarlane, *Witchcraft in Tudor and Stuart England*; K. Thomas, *Religion and the decline of Magic*; C. Ginzburg, *The Night Battles: Witchcraft and Agrarian Cults in the Sixteenth and Seventeenth Centuries*.; A. Gurevich, *Medieval Popular Culture: Problems of Belief and Perception*.; R. Horsley, 'Who were the witches? The social roles of the accused in the European witch trials', pp.689-715; C. Larner, '*Crimen exceptum*? The crime of witchcraft in Europe', pp.49-75.

she should hang a silver amulet around the neck of a virgin girl.
When she went to confession, the priest would not absolve her and
directed her to confess the matter to the Inquisitor.[2] In explaining
the character and content of the accusations and confessions, we
also need to take into account the historical processes of mediation
between the different cultural levels of a complex society, such as
obtained in early modern Malta.

As in the rest of Mediterranean Europe, particularly southern
Italy, the chief concern of the Inquisition tribunal was to reform
popular witchcraft beliefs, making them conform to official notions
of religion as proposed by the Council of Trent. Since 'ideas of the
victimless crime, sin in the mind and truth by self-accusation' could
not produce penance[3] traditional forms of justice often held sway in
the inquisitorial and episcopal courts. Hence restitutive justice was
often conceived as penance. Thus although the Roman Inquisition –
in contrast to the Spanish – was far more concerned with illicit
magic – a crime that included witchcraft – neither of them treated
the matter with great severity. Nonetheless, witchcraft accusations
abounded and, according to surviving records, there were even a few
mass accusations of witches in the early seventeenth century. It
accounts for the reason why the Inquisition was most active during
the early decades of the seventeenth century.[4] It even suggests an
increased role of the Inquisitor and his tribunal in the prosecution
of *maleficium*. Yet the activities of the Inquisition against crimes of
witchcraft and sorcery contrast strikingly with the severity of
secular judges in northern Europe. The Holy Office was somewhat
dubious of the efficacy of 'superstitious magic', and consequently
suspects were treated with relative leniency.[5]

This lack of severity held sway thanks to the common view that
witchcraft was derived from a residual 'pagan superstition and

---

2 AIM Proc Crim. 18, case 214, fol.195: 24 May 1599.

3 J. Bossy, *Christianity in the West*, 1400-1700, p. 139.

4 W. Monter & J. Tedeschi, 'Toward a statistical profile of the Italian Inquisitions, sixteenth to
   eighteenth centuries', p.146. A few mass trials took place in Malta during the first quarter of
   the seventeenth century. C. Cassar, 'Witchcraft beliefs and social control', p.329.

5 W. Monter, *Ritual, Myth and Magic in Early Modern Europe*, p.66-7.

ignorance', rather than diabolical apostasy – a view with roots in the ninth-century *Canon episcopi*.[6] This mode of reasoning was coupled with reluctance to the use of torture, the importance attached to centralized control, and to the assigning of little weight to denunciations made by accused witches. This approach is best explained in the *'Instructo pro formandis processibus in causis strigum, sortilegiorum, et maleficiorum'* which J. Tedeschi considers as the 'fullest and most eloquent expression' of the tribunal's responsible attitude.[7] The *Instructo,* first circulated in manuscript form among the provincial tribunals of the Inquisition, appeared in print for the first time in 1625 – when it was published in the second edition of Eliseo Masini's *Sacro Arsenale.* It was only published in pamphlet form in 1657 without any reference to the illegal meddling of the secular magistrates. As J. Tedeschi explains, this may have been done in order to avoid compounding the conflict with the secular courts, who at the time were accusing the Holy Office of laxity in prosecuting witchcraft, while contesting its jurisdiction and augmenting the severity of their own procedures.[8]

It is interesting to observe that the General Inquisition in Rome kept close scrutiny over instances of severity and haste by local tribunals, partly due to the lingering impact of the *Malleus Maleficarum.* In the correspondence of the Holy Office, one meets frequent counsels for care in gathering evidence, in particular before imprisoning, torturing or handing a suspect over to the Holy Office.[9] In a 1608 letter written by Cardinal Arrigoni, a senior cardinal of the Holy Office, to Inquisitor della Corbara in Malta – in response to procedural questions arising from the treatment of the octogenerian 'witch' Betta Caloiro – Arrigoni suggests that since Betta abjured from her 'heretical' practices, she should be allowed to live the rest of her days in relative peace. Furthermore

---

6 D. Gentilcore, *From Bishop to Witch*, p.241.

7 J. Tedeschi, 'The Roman Inquisition and Witchcraft: an early seventeenth-century "Instruction" on correct trial procedure', p.188.

8 Ibid., p.176.

9 G. Bonomo, *Caccia alle Streghe: La Credenza nelle Streghe dal Sec. XIII al XIX con Particolare Riferimento all'Italia*, p.295-97.

the Inquisitor had to ensure that Betta would not die without confessing.[10] A few months later Betta passed away in the Inquisitor's prison and was denied Catholic burial; so that she was buried in unconsecrated ground at the Palace. After further consultation with other members of the Holy Congregation, Arrigoni insisted that Betta should be re-buried in sacred ground.[11] The letter-writing activity of the Cardinal secretary of the General Tribunal in Rome testifies to the centralizing concern of the Holy Office in maintaining the judicial propriety of its provincial branches, even where it operated through an Inquisition Tribunal as in early modern Malta. For instance, in response to a query of 1608 regarding the large amount of magical writings which were confiscated and kept at the Holy Office, the Cardinal – somewhat patronisingly – advised Inquisitor Leonetto della Corbara, that from then on such writings should be burned, once the case was concluded.[12] There are numerous letters like the above, on all aspects of the running the Tribunal, some almost sarcastic in tone, in which the Secretary to the General Tribunal in Rome answered endless queries on procedure, or adviced on sentencing by instructing local officials what had to be treated as routine business, and what not. The same concern is manifest in the many sentences sent to Rome by local inquisitions for confirmation or revision.

Maleficium and Accusations of Diabolical Witchcraft

Because the charge of diabolical witchcraft was based on a criminalization of a set of magical activities, the suspects were not selected at random, but in general had *a prior* reputation for *maleficium*, based on the recognition of a series of more or less

---

[10] AIM Corr.I (part ii) fol.321: 8 August 1608.

[11] Cardinal Arrigoni sent two letters to Inquisitor della Corbara on the matter. The first one dated 6 December 1608: Ibid., fol.345; the second dated 9 January, 1609:Ibid., Corr. II, fol.5.

[12] Ibid., fol.323: 23 August 1608.

public 'performances': blessings, incantations, curses and manipulations. As a result, various levels of labelling were employed by neighbours which, depending on other factors, might or might not result in a formal accusation before the court.[13] One can safely assume that Malta – similar to Europe – passed through a witch craze between the late sixteenth and early seventeenth centuries. In accounting for the rise in similar accusations against suspected witches, the presence of the courts themselves should not be underestimated. Often such reactions were pushed 'from below'. In a deposition against Sulpitia de Lango – accused of having prepared a magic potion in the Conventual Church of the Order of St John – the knight Fra Sanese Sanesi explained how both the knights and people present had suggested that de Lango should be burned at the stake, since she had been so often accused of witchcraft at the Holy Office.[14] It explains why J. Bossy remarks that there was 'a greater willingness to bring to court, disputes where witchcraft was suspected'.[15]

As far as the Church was concerned, the possession of a bad reputation or 'fame' – the *malafama* – constituted a virtual crime in itself, so that it was almost always mentioned in conjunction with charges of illicit magic.[16] Common too were links with moral shortcomings, like 'filthy behaviour' or religious deviance, blasphemy or absence from Church attendance. This explains why someone, like Joanne Falsone of Qormi, could denounce the physician Mattheo Cassia as being 'regarded by the majority of the people of the village as a scoundrel'. Besides Cassia was reputed to have had carnal relations with his god-mother Margarita Schembri. Furthermore, he had even spent seven years in Lutheran states where he

---

[13] C. Larner, '*Crimen exceptum*', p.52.

[14] AIM Proc Crim. 38A case 302, fol.11v: 29 June 1617.

[15] J. Bossy, *Christianity in the West*, p.78.

[16] The phrase 'common whore and witch' was also used in the same way throughout England. A. Macfarlane, *Witchcraft in Tudor and Stuart England: A Regional and Comparative Study*, pp.277-79.

had participated in warfare. Worse still, Falsone accused Cassia of never having seen him go to confession and in fact of having noted him at mass only once at the village church since his return from the wars.[17]

The increasing activity of the Inquisition tribunal in the decades following the Council of Trent does not alone suffice to account for the number of accusations made before it. As one will have occasion to observe in later chapters, most of the cases concerning 'magic and superstition' were initiated from below. One fantastic denunciation was put forward by Valerio Cauchi, who stated that by 1599 he had been living in the Gozo Castello for about twenty years. Cauchi declared how Isabetta Caruana, a reputed *magara*, was often referred to by other women as *trista donna e magara* (sorrowful woman and witch). In order to confirm this hearsay, Cauchi reported how three or four years before, while looking out of his terrace, he had seen two nude women riding, like mad, on broomsticks in the air and he recognised them as Isabetta and her daughter Romana, a public prostitute. Cauchi was so sure that he had seen the two women flying, that he even mentioned the names of several other persons who had witnessed the same scene.[18] In a similar case Nella Gat alias *di Bohrot* accused Agatha Xellula of being a *donna corteggiana publica* (public prostitute) and a *gran trista vigliacca e magara* (a very gloomy coward and witch). Nella *di Bohrot* thus linked sorcery with prostitution, another negative attribute, and the object of public talk and rife rumour circulating among the people in the Gozo Citadel.[19]

This picture seems to have been true throughout Europe, independent of whether the accusations culminated in a large-scale witch-hunt or whether individual scapegoats were singled out. Since witchcraft was essentially an imagined crime, the initial stages of accusation and prosecution were thus the most important in attempting to determine the contributing factors, with the result that a qualitative study of the trial records is potentially more

---

[17] AIM Proc Crim. 17 case 151 fol.402: 19 February 1600.

[18] Ibid., 147A, case 83 (item 4), fol.56: 14 June 1599.

[19] Ibid., 19B, case 46, fol.411.

revealing than a quantitative one. Furthermore the trial records do not always give us the information we need (such as age, marital status, occupation, dealings with neighbours), so that our interpretation of the social dynamics leading to accusations must be based on a relatively small sample of cases.[20]

The Devil: Betta Caloiro and Farfarello

The standard explanation favoured by demonologists for women's attraction for the devil was their insatiable lust. In a case of demonic obsession, Betta Caloiro called the devil *farfarello*[21] who appeared in the shape of a 'six year old boy', dressed in clothes of several colours, who often visited her at night. She asserted that in her youth, several people told her that these visions were due to a missing word in her baptism. The first time she met *farfarello* was at the age of six when she was living near the *giardino di Sant' Helena* at Burmola and had been instructed to carry some bowls of food to an elderly relative. *Farfarello* appeared at the head of a band of little devils carrying a club, with which he hit her on the neck, so that she remained ill for six months after the incident. She asserted that a priest – Don Pietro Ros, curate of the church of St Helen at Burmola, before the siege of 1565 – suggested that she should prepare the table with food and cutlery every day, so that *farfarello* and his friends would let her live in peace.[22]

On 25 June, 1601, in the course of her second interrogation, Betta Caloiro recalled how she had had an intimate relationship with the devil *farfarello* since the age of twelve. One would notice that Betta changed some details from her earlier deposition of 22 August 1600, regarding the first encounter with *farfarello*:

---

[20] B. P. Levack, *The Witch-Hunt*, p.117.

[21] G. Pitrè writing in the late nineteenth century points out, that in popular belief, devils were looked upon essentially as tricksters who caused trouble. In Sicily *Farfareddu* – or *farfarello* as referred to by Dante Alighieri in the *Divine Comedy* (Hell cantos 21 & 22) – is a nocturnal devil who disturbs the minds and hearts of men. Yet the demon can only disturb people who were baptised incompletely, that is to say, those who had some words omitted from the ritual or were baptised without the adoperation of oil or salt. G. Pitrè, *Usi e Costumi*, Vol.4, p.74.

[22] AIM Proc Crim. 19B case 46, fols. 477a-77av.

When I was a twelve year old girl, I was living at Burmola near the garden of St Helen. One day I was cooking cabbage soup and I was hit by a strong wind in my neck... – from which it took me around four months to recover – and I imme diately saw six young boys wearing frilled clothes of different colours and that evening I prepared bread and left it in a wooden box which I kept at home. At night, while I was sleeping, I heard intense noises coming from the house and having woken up, I heard the munching of eating in such a way that it seemed as if a large number of people were eating. When I went to check in the morning I found no bread left in the house... When I spoke to my neighbour about the matter, she told me that they were *fati* (fairies) and suggested that I should prepare the table for them with a plate of white honey, salt, knife, bread, wine and water. The following morning I found all the bread they had taken away from me the previous night...

When Betta went to inform her neighbour about this new development, she found her neighbour in the company of a *fato* – looking like a young boy – who was weaving for her. She added that this *fato* had in fact woven sixty *canne* of linen within the short span of eight days.[23]

In another deposition Betta could assert, 'farfarello is not a devil because he has a lot of friends and they must be fairies who appear at night and I invoke them in order to honour them...' Later she added, 'in truth when I invoke him (*farfarello*) I recite the *Ave Maria* and the *Pater Noster* in order to honour and thank him and make him act without delay'.[24]

Taken in context, it would seem that old women, like Betta Caloiro, nurtured sexual fantasies which expressed a desire on the part of the women to transcend their own condition. Significantly, the devil offers all sorts of things, such as money and magical powers.[25] The victims of these temptations were almost always

---

[23] Ibid., fols.494v-95: 25 June, 1601.

[24] Ibid., fols.480v-81: 23 August, 1600.

[25] G. Pitrè asserts that the devil of oral culture in Sicily, '*non è il diavolo comunemente inteso... ma bensì quello che era talora nel medioevo, un essere indefinito nella magia, nella stregoneria, che misfà per propria volontà o per altrui. Il suo superiore non è Dio, come nel diavolo o demonio della religione e delle credenze cristiane, ma un mago, uno stregone potente e strapotente*'. *Fiabe, Novelle e Racconti del Popolo Siciliano*, vol.I. p.cxxiii.

poor, helpless women, and the devil's promises were closely related to their plight, giving us little reason to doubt the reality of such fantasies.[26] Thus Betta recalled how previous to the siege of 1565, she had made the acquaintance of a woman from Żebbug, called Ginaina, who became rich since a group of *fati* helped her produce large amounts of linen. Indeed Ginaina became so rich that she did not have enough space were to keep the money. One morning Betta went to ask her for fire and noticed that Ginaina had already prepared the table. The table was covered with a clean white tablecloth, and laid with bread, salt, honey and a knife. Betta wondered why Ginaina had prepared her lunch so early. On asking her next door neighbour, a woman called *Xellusa*, Betta was told that Ginaina prepared a meal for the *fati* who helped her produce so much linen.[27] Even more common was the hoped for satisfaction of their economic needs, not surprising, considering that many of the accused witches were weak and helpless, with no other means of power or influence.

Temptations could also be induced by religious fear and despair, such as the lack of hope in salvation. This tells us something of the nature of religious instruction – and perhaps of the ability of oral culture to shift orthodox beliefs to suit one's own psychological needs – that the devil frequently promised to pay women's debts and lead them into heaven. Thus Betta invoked *farfarello* with the words: *O farfarello Salomone vieni* (Oh Farfarello Salomon come) and invariably he came to the rescue of his friend Betta![28] Later Betta admitted that she treated *farfarello* like a saint whom she revered,[29] although on several occasions she asserted readiness to repent and return back to the folds of the Catholic Church.[30] On 22

---

[26] K. Thomas, *Religion and the Decline of Magic*, pp.621-28.

[27] According to Betta, Ginaina became so attached to her wealth that during the siege of 1565 she left beleagured Birgu to recover her goods at Żebbug; she was caught by the Turks, and no one heard about her whereabouts since. AIM Proc Crim. 19B case 46, fol.490-91: 15 October, 1600.

[28] Ibid., 19B case 46, fols.477v-77a.

[29] Ibid., fol.495v.

[30] See for example: Ibid., fol.486: 2 September, 1600; Ibid., fol.496: 25 June, 1601. On one occasion she admitted that by honouring and invoking the devil, one goes against the teachings of the church, since one should only honour God and his saints. Ibid., fol.488v.

July, 1601 Betta abjured, wearing the penitential habit with a candle in hand, in a ceremony staged at the Annunciation Church in Vittoriosa. She was condemned to eight years imprisonment and ordered to confess once a month and recite the rosary every Saturday for the following two years.[31] Yet she continued to invoke her friend *farfarello* even some years later, while held in the Inquisitor's prison. On one occasion she was overheard by the prison warden, Antonio Napolitano, to exclaim: *Merchiba Merchiba bich harusi ma tigix tarani, ena hauni carcerata haij chasara.*[32]

It seems that successive inquisitors were not at all convinced that Betta had really repented from her old ways, and it seems that every now and then she spent some time imprisoned at the Inquisitor's palace.[33]

Confessions, including admissions of invocation to devils by the accused were at most times nothing more than the fruits of delusion, hysteria and melancholy. A state of depression characterized such odd behaviour in women that G.R. Quaife was lead to suggest that not only did such confessions reflect the misogynistic theories of demonologists, but also reflected the unsatisfied sexual needs of accused women. Possibly the sexual habits of the early modern males may have further contributed to such a state of affairs: these do not seem to have engaged in fore and after-play, enabling the devil to bring 'pleasure into the dull lives of disturbed, bored and frustrated women, even if only in imagination'.[34] H.C.E. Midelfort's study of early modern Germany yields similar conclusions.

---

[31] Ibid., fols. 500-502v, 487v.

[32] English translation: 'Welcome, welcome to you, my betrothed/ you do not come to see me/ I am imprisoned here/ alas!'Ibid., 24A case 2, fol.10: 8 August, 1605.

[33] Due to her old age Betta was kept at her sister's house in Birgu. On 19 February, 1607 she was taken to the Monastery of St Scholastica. Meanwhile she apparently spent several periods of time in prison as when she invoked *farfarello* in 1605. She died in prison due to her old age on 6 September, 1608. Ibid., 28C case 227, fol.1237v. Full text reproduced in Appendix I below.

[34] G.R. Quaife, *Godly Zeal and Furious Rage: The Witch in Early Modern Europe*, pp.99-102.

Many women in their confessions emphasized that they were seduced into witchcraft when they were sad, dejected or even desperate.[35]

The failure to fulfill the functions of wife and mother unleashed a general hostility to women which could in turn generate severe depression. This was particularly applicable to widows and senile women.[36]

At the same time, the devil played an ambivalent role in popular culture, where rather than being the personification of evil, the devil had more the semblance of a demon. In the confessions, extracted by the Inquisition he appears 'more as a legendary figure of folklore than as the master of a demonic cult'.[37] Indeed some of the narratives have a distinctly folktale-like quality. In 1608 Inziana Paradisi, a seventy year old Greek widow and wise woman who specialized in healing babies, declared that she was often visited by male and female *folletti*[38] which she could recognize because the males wore a beard and females wore feminine clothes. She could even describe the colours of their vestments, asserting that they were obsessed with cleanliness. According to her deposition, Inziana was visited by these *folletti* at night. On one occasion, some twenty years earlier, Inziana had a terrible experience with one of these *folletti*. She had been sleeping in the flickering light of a candle and as she spit, she accidentally hit a *folletto* who was passing by. The *folletto* became so angry that he tried to spit in her mouth. The *folletto* disappeared once she made the sign of the cross. Inziana recalled how she was first visited by a *folletto* when she was fourteen. He was wearing a red cap and white clothes and

[35] H.C.E. Midelfort, 'The social position of the witch in south western Germany', pp.181-82.

[36] Betta Caloiro apparently had both problems. In October 1599 she declared that she was then about eighty years old and had been a widow for the last sixteen years. AIM Crim., 19B case 46 fol.453.

[37] R. Kieckhefer, *European Witch Trials: Their Foundations in Popular and Learned Culture, 1300-1500*, p.36.

[38] According to G. Pitrè, the *folletto* is a good little devil who was not punished by God, like all the other rebel devils. He is not evil minded but rather witty, whimsical and bizarre and enjoys himself making people lose their patience, particularly during their prayers. *Usi e Costumi*, Vol.4, pp.77-8.

continued to visit her every night, so much so that, when her husband was absent, he even teased her in bed and took off her clothes.[39]

Such folktale motifs, as an integral part of a belief system, were naturally adapted and utilized in this way in interpersonal contacts at the local level, thus finding their way into witchcraft accusations. Some folk beliefs had relevance in the daily existence of the largely peasant populations of pre-industrial societies. Others could have served other purposes and may not have been directly relevant to everyday life.[40] Yet there seems little doubt that those accused believed what they were confessing. None the less, it would seem that the devil remained 'un-diabolized' in the popular culture of early modern times. As J. Delumeau puts it,

> That Christianity should undergo a process of folklorisation and pagan- isation was hardly avoidable in a civilisation where education was a rare commodity, technological and scientific know-how in short supply and consequently the fear of hunger, the threat of the elements, the imminence of sickness and death everywhere rampant.[41]

Likewise, the accused not only recounted their version, in the form of confession, but they also 'drew on local folklore in an attempt to satisfy their questioners' demands for a complete account of the significance of their actions'.[42] These dynamics came into play whenever a local *magara* boasted of her powers to her neighbours, or when the same woman – or her neighbours, as witnesses – were obliged to relate and re-articulate the event to the legal men in authority.[43]

Finally the witchcraft narratives recounted to the Malta Inquisition give insights into the way the tribunal managed to impose itself on all sectors of public and private life. Above all, it managed to manipulate the minds of the ordinary folk, by adapting

---

[39] AIM Crim., 28C case 227, fol.1286v: 28 September, 1608.

[40] R. Kieckhefer, *Witch Trials*, p.40.

[41] J. Delumeau, Catholicism between Luther and Voltaire, pp.168-69.

[42] R. Rowland, '"Fantasticall and devilishe persons"', p.181.

[43] V. Turner, 'Social dramas and stories about them', pp.155-58.

testimonies to its own 'notions and theological preoccupations'.[44] This explains why P. Burke rightly reminds us that the archives accomodated the needs of the literate few, hence our knowledge of the ordinary people is passed to us 'via records made for the most part, by members of the cultural élite'.[45]

Maleficium and Social Relations

Accusations and trials for the casting of spells seeking to cause bodily harm to people, as well as animals, or some other tribulation were certainly the most common forms of *maleficium*. Techniques included image or homeopathic magic, the placing of magical substances close to the intended victim, and the recitation of incantations, usually in conjunction with the first two methods.

Domenico Borg of Mosta recalled how in September 1598 he saw a woman dressed in white walking out of his courtyard. Apparently his wife had not seen anyone entering her house. The next morning, his bitch fell ill and died within three days. Soon after his cat died. Then it was the turn of his pregnant jenny who miscarried and died a few days later. Finally it was his wife's turn to feel sick. She refrained from eating and drinking, threw him out of their home, accusing him of being the devil incarnate, and even declared that her husband was long dead.[46] Evidently Domenico Borg was certain that his household had been struck by the worst kind of evil.

Divinatory magic was also important. Its relationship to forms of sorcery was often complementary, given that knowledge of a particular situation might lead to a desire to take some form of magical action. In this way, it provided the weak and powerless with a means of maintaining relative stability in their lives, at least psychologically. For this reason poor women often made use of beneficent and maleficient magic.

---

[44] C. Ginzburg, *The Night Battles*, pp.11-12.

[45] P. Burke, *The Historical Anthropology of Early Modern Italy*, p.79.

[46] AIM Proc Crim. 18 case 208, fol.174: 8 April, 1600.

Maleficium, like the impotence-causing ligature, was frequently the reverse side of popular healing, in as much as it was often the supposed source of ailments requiring ritual cure. Damiano Cassar of Gozo accused his carnal friend Agatha, alias Xellula, of having practised magic to cause him impotence if he frequented other women. He asserted how he learned from hearsay that women who practice magic, *donne fattuchiare*, often make use of potions and enchantments that help create impotence. Thus when asked, Agatha confessed that she had asked Margarita Zammit, alias *Mineichiret*, to bewitch him.[47] Margarita Zammit appears to have acquired the reputation of a witch in Gozo. Several men and women accused her of all sorts of *maleficium*, ranging from bewitchment to impotence-causing ligature and its cure, to that of procuress and prostitute. Amongst others, Clara, wife of Stephano d'Antonio, had sought her assistance to remove the ligature of her husband.[48]

Lauria Mangion also declared Margarita to be a practising witch.[49] At the same time, Domenico Carceppo accused her of having acted as procuress between the medical doctor Francesco Turrense and Lauria, his still virgin sister-in-law. Thanks to the magical machinations of Margarita Zammit, Turrense managed to enjoy the company of Lauria for a couple of months, an affair that was terminated only after Carceppo had quarrelled bitterly with Turrense over the matter.[50] The evidence put forward by Margarita herself is significant as it allows us to gain insight on how certain women served as scapegoats in a society where insecurity and survival were the order of the day. In her evidence of 24 June 1599, Margarita referred to an incident that occurred seven years before, thanks to which she indirectly managed to gain the reputation of a witch. She had been severly beaten, had her clothes torn and threatened with being knifed by her first husband. She was so terrorized, that she climbed up the terrace and decided to leap into

---

[47] AIM Proc Crim. 19B case 46 fol.397-v: 5 May 1599.
[48] Ibid., fol.396: 6 May, 1599.
[49] Ibid., fol.415: 16 June, 1599.
[50] Ibid., fol.415v: 16 June 1599.

her neighbour's house. But before she jumped off, Margarita made the sign of the cross. A woman, who saw her crossing herself before jumping, denounced her to the Inquisition for practising witch-craft.[51] The resort to magic and the resulting accusation thus appear as elements in expressing social tensions.

Apart from being a means of explaining and regulating awkward or inappropriate relationships, sorcery accusations could be employed to incriminate people. Since the victim could use the spell as a means of face-saving among his or her neighbours, so, conversely, magic was a means of causing the 'loss of face' in others accused of employing it. Frequently those accused of other crimes were also identified as *fattuchiari* to present them in a worse light to the Inquisition, for this had the effect of inflating the bad repu-tation of the accused. Petruccia Vassallo was supposedly a good friend of Agatha *alias* Xellula so much so that Agatha confided some of her secrets with her. Amongst other Agatha told Petruccia that she had approached Betta Caloiro[52] in order to effect an impo-tence ligature on her lover Damiano Cassar.[53] Unfortunately Petruccia gave Agatha away to Nella Gat *alias* di Bohrot. Petruccia warned Nella to avoid Agatha by declaring that she was both a prostitute and a witch.[54] Another acquaintance of Agatha, Julia Bonnici alias *di Marzo*, further complicated matters by claiming that Agatha must have learned a lot of remedies from her close relationship with Betta Caloiro and Margarita Zammit. This was a very serious accusation since the two women were notorious for their *magarie* (witchcraft) among the inhabitants of Gozo.[55]

Instead of trying to defend her position, Agatha preferred to put herself in bad light. In her deposition Agatha not only admitted her close relationship with these women, but she even explained how Betta Caloiro taught her to adoperate sorcery. As if this was not

---

[51] Ibid., fols. 423-24.

[52] Betta Caloiro, Margarita Zammit, and a healer from Mqabba called Marietta, were all known as *mineichiret* due to the fact that they had a twisted nose. Evidence suggests that this was the result of venereal ailment.

[53] Ibid., fol.408v.

[54] Ibid., fol.411.

[55] Ibid., fol.410.

enough, Agatha went so far as to declare that she had invoked the devil – during the celebration of mass at the Augustinian church in Rabat, Gozo – and offered him her body and soul. Yet she regretted having done so and spent a restless night terrified at the thought of having any dealings with the devil. Agatha's very bad reputation was at the root of all her troubles. Thus although she tried to confess her sins to various Gozitan priests, the Curate of the Matrix Church would scold any priest who tried to hear her confession since Agatha had a notorious reputation as prostitute.[56] The negative reputation she had attained as prostitute was so strong that her close friend and notorious witch, Betta Caloiro was ready to disclaim any dealings with Agatha. Betta went so far as to ask the Inquisitor, 'Would you believe prostitutes rather than myself?'[57]

But who were these wise women, these *magare*? First of all they were women who, apart from the customary roles of cook, healer and midwife, were believed to have a direct connection with the practice of *maleficium*. Moreover, despite the informal power relationships so crucial to village and town life, women found it more difficult to defend themselves and their interests, and so more frequently turned to sorcery as a means of doing so – or were naturally suspected of employing it for this purpose.[58] The gender bias present in accusations of sorcery and witchcraft might also reflect a struggle among women for control of the feminine space, possibly intensified by the number of unmarried women lacking familial support.[59] The fact that many women suspected of sorcery were widows may be explained as evidence that such women lacked the protection of a husband, whose presence could exert influence in containing rumours.[60]

Similar attitudes are evident in tribal society. Among the Nupe of Nigeria, for example, witch hunting is related to a period when

---

[56] Ibid., fol.420-21v: 24 June 1599.

[57] Ibid., fol.457: 14 October, 1599.

[58] B. P. Levack, *The Witch-hunt in Early Modern Europe*, p.108.

[59] G.R. Quaife, *Godly Zeal and Furious Rage: The Witch in Early Modern Europe*, p.108.

[60] C. Cassar, 'Witchcraft beliefs and social control'; Ibid. 'Popular beliefs and perceptions in Hospitaller Malta', pp.460-70.

women take over the roles of men as traders in the economy. This results in an inversion of roles since these women violate the norms of caring submissive females, as they take on lovers, lead an independent life, travel widely and rarely produce heirs. The only efficient way to control them is by accusing them of witchcraft.[61] Similarly in the highly patriarchal societies of the past – as in the case of early modern Malta – women, who were subject to the control of neither father nor husband, were a source of suspicion and even fear.[62] It may also be true that there was a tendency to suspect healers and cunning women of sorcery, as old age brought on increasingly eccentric or anti-social behaviour, making neighbours uncomfortable. At the same time, their advanced age increased their chances of being widowed.

Another characteristic frequently shared by accused *magare* was poverty. Although not usually the poorest members of society – the itinerant poor – they frequently lived at subsistence level, many having to beg to survive. As such, they were weak and vulnerable, and often depended on both beneficent and maleficent magic to sustain both their precarious status and financial standing. They were often the ones suspected of having invoked or made a pact with the Devil – being considered the most likely to resort to such a step. And because such women were dependent on their local community, whether rural or urban, they could easily arouse resentment and even a sense of guilt amongst their neighbours. Thus the resulting accusation could be either an attempt at legitimate retaliation, or a projection of the guilt experienced by the accusers on to the accused. In this regard, it has been suggested that a general decline in the standard of living may have made neighbours less tolerant in dealing with the poor and more prepared to rely on accusations of sorcery in order to maintain their position in society.[63] However, this must be seen against a background of increased vigilance on the part of the ecclesiastical courts

---

[61] S.F. Nadel, *Nupe Religion*, pp.163-81.

[62] C. Cassar, 'Witchcraft beliefs and social control', pp.328-29.

[63] B. P. Levack, *The Witch-hunt in Early Modern Europe*, p.129.

and the influence of preachers and confessors in convincing people of the evils of *maleficium*, typical of the two centuries following the Council of Trent.

In Malta devil-worshipping appears to have played a very minor role at a popular level, so that the allegation of 'a pact with the devil' was often vague and peripheral to the main accusation put forward in the majority of witchcraft cases. Indeed the most complicated case where the accused confessed to have had carnal relations with the Devil is that of Geltrude Navarra, heard by Inquisitor Pignatelli. It was such a unique and extraordinary case, that the Inquisition tribunal kept it as a separate volume.[64]

Where no tangible harm resulted, or where the Inquisition was faced with a lack of evidence, the inquisitors were instructed to punish those denounced of such accusations with a light penance.[65] As I.M. Lewis observed, it is

> by being overcome involuntarily by an arbitrary affliction for which they cannot be held accountable, these possessed women gain attention and consideration and, within variously defined limits, successfully manoeuvre their husbands and menfolk.[66]

Popular witchcraft beliefs were the outcome of church indoctrination and obsession to extricate all forms of heresy and the works of the Devil – an all important and omnipotent character in popular religious cosmology.

---

[64] The case of Geltrude Navarra is summarised by A. Bonnici in, *Il-Maltin u l-Inkizizzjoni f'Nofs is-Seklu Sbatax*, pp.103-5.

[65] AIM Misc.2 p.30.

[66] I.M. Lewis, *Ecstatic Religion: An Anthropological Study of Spirit Possession and Shamanism*, p.77.

Popular Healing Rituals

Throughout the late sixteenth and the seventeenth centuries, the Catholic Church intensified efforts to eliminate current notions of popular religion. But as the ex-consultant of the Malta Inquisition Tribunal, the Jesuit Sebastiano Salelles remarks, 'Inquisition proceedings against magic spread by infidels, prostitutes and witches will hardly ever come to an end'.[1]

Salelles's point of view coincides with the position of the Tridentine Church's effort to eradicate various aspects of popular belief at a time when forms of ritualized response to malady and misfortune functioned largely outside both the Church's liturgical framework and the realms of learned medicine. The popular ritual included formulaic invocations and conjurations to treat both human and animal illnesses of all kinds. Such activities, were often restricted to a community of healers, or *magare* who frequently attempted to establish a direct contact with religion outside ecclesiastical structures.

This crude practical use of religious ritual helped to trans form Christian devotions into functional magic. The Church itself after the Council of Trent, continued to encourage the use of ritual to convince the people of its effectiveness. This mentality was so deeply felt that anyone who doubted such theories could be denounced to the Inquisition. Mastro Blasio Zammit, for example, was denounced by a neighbour for having ridiculed the carrying in procession of the statue of St Agatha on the walls of Mdina, at the time of the 1551 siege.[2]

---

1 S. Salelles, *De Materiis Tribunalium S. Inquisitionis*, p.62.

2 AIM Proc Crim. 3B, case 63, fols 622-25: 18 June, 1574.

Invocations also made use of the names and power of saints, often considered as patrons for specific ailments such as St Lucy (the eyes), St Roque (plague), St Margaret (pregnancy). For this reason they overlap with the Church-approved and often Church-sponsored devotions to saints and their relics. Such popular devotions formed a pool of remedies which patients could dip into at times of physical or psychological need. They gave the individual confidence in the face of fear and provided an outlet for hostility, by attempting to explain misfortune or failure while revealing the causes of illness.

Official and Popular Medicine

One characteristic of medicinal cures at this period was its pluralism. As there was a saint for practically every malady, so too there was a variety of specialists for specific complaints, such as bone-setters (*concia ossi*), surgeons or barbers.[3] The latter were considered somewhere between the physician or the apothecary (*aromatario*) and the more popular practitioners, like folk healers, whilst for women in labour there was the midwife.[4] Quack healers were frequently condemned by both official medicine and Church exorcists. The Church went so far as to condemn all types of popular healers, since they sought independent access to the supernatural. Such an activity had a potentially diabolical origin and was seen as the outcome of an expressed or tacit pact with the devil.

Yet witch beliefs were widespread at a time when medical knowledge was often inadequate. Even within the realm of folk medicine, there was what modern medicine might consider a surprising amount of variety. As elsewhere in Europe, techniques and rituals varied greatly, from traditional folk remedies, predominantly herbal, to

---

[3] P. Burke, *The Historical Anthropology of Early Modern Italy*, p.208.

[4] See for example: L. B. Pinto, 'The folk practice of gynaecology and obstetrics in the Middle Ages', pp.513-22; T. R. Forbes, 'The regulation of English midwives in the sixteenth and seventeenth centuries', pp.235-44; T. G. Benedeck, 'The changing relationship between midwives and physicians during the Renaissance', pp.550-64; C Savona Ventura, 'The influence of the Roman Catholic Church on midwifery practice in Malta', pp. 18-34.

prayers and invocations either accompanying the medicine, or even forming the sole means of treatment. Magic was connected with the traditional medicine of the healer, particularly the female healer.[5] Such popular healers, particularly old women, were to be found in many parts of Europe under different names but using similar techniques. In England, remarks Burke,

> they were known as... 'wise women', in Spain as *saludadores* (healers), in Sicily as *giravoli* (wanderers)... They treated with herbs... and not least with a variety of charms, prayers and rituals in which candles and (in Catholic countries) even consecrated wafers had their part.[6]

Perna Cachialepre of Vittoriosa recalled how, a couple of years earlier, a certain Antonina suggested that she should consult a Maltese female acquaintance called Nuasia from Senglea *che sapeva guarire molte infirmità* (who knew how to heal many ailments). She even consulted Minica, another Senglea healer, who knew how to heal the evil eye.[7] Similarly, Marietta alias Nasca, daughter of Blasio Zammit, *faceva la professione di medicar molte sorte di infirmità* (practised the healing profession to cure many diseases).[8] The same could be said of Marietta alias *mineichiret* of Mqabba,[9] an unnamed old woman known as *di Merlin* from Lija,[10] and Margarita Fiteni, an old Sicilian woman living at Tarxien.[11]

---

5 E. Le Roy Ladurie attributes this phenomenon to the scarcity of literacy among females who 'thus became the preserves of natural, non-scholastic culture, and also more and more suspect to the men. And mistrust of women soon turned into suspicion of witchcraft'. *Montaillou*, p.343.

6 P. Burke, *Popular Culture in Early Modern Europe*, p.106.

7 AIM Proc Crim. 18, case 227 fol.237-v: 9 April, 1599.

8 Ibid., 146, item 5 (case 76), fol.114; 14 July 1599.

9 Ibid., 18 case 223, fol.224v: 24 December 1599.

10 '*mi dissero alcuni... che detta mia figlia non sarra mai guarita se io non la facessi guarire da una donna del casal Lia vechia decrepita qual non so suo nome, ma era chiamata da tutti, di Merlin, la qual al presente è morta*'. (some people told me.. that my daughter would not heal if I do not take her to an old decrepit woman from Lija, whose name is unknown to me, but who is called by everyone as *di Merlin*, and she is now dead.) Ibid., Vol. 16A case 34 fol.249: 28 December 1598.

11 '*...intendo dire nel nostro casale Luca che nel casale Tarxen vi sia una donna vecchia Siciliana chiamata Margarita Fiteni la quale, sa guarire li putti d'ogni male*'. (I hear people in Luqa say that at Tarxien there is an old Sicilian woman called Margarita Fiteni who knows how to heal babies from every illness') Ibid., 23A, case 321, fol.323: 18 June 1601.

Healing was part of the female sphere, since the realtionship with the body – vis-à-vis disease and reproduction – formed part of what were considered the feminine sphere and its responsibilities. I.M. Lewis asserts that,

> there is no doubt that in many, if not most societies, women are in fact treated as peripheral creatures. The peripherality of women in this sense is… a general feature of all those societies in which men hold a secure monopoly of the major power positions and deny their partners effective jural equality. …the treatment of women as marginal persons denies, or at least ignores, their fundamental biosocial importance and in social terms clashes with their deep committment to a particular culture and society.[12]

Women used magical language in order to help build up emotion al tensions in particular situations, while the spells, ritual acts and gestures kept up a tense flow of emotions.[13] They include the mumbling of a few words either upon the afflicted part of the body or to 'enchant' a clothing item usually worn by the patient.

The Carmelite tertiary, *soro* Ventura Busuttil of Żejtun, went to seek advice from the notorious healer Betta Caloiro in order to cure her unmarried brother, Andrea Busuttil, from the baneful influence of the evil eye. The brother had allegedly spent his fortune on prostitutes and pledged his damask clothes in order to acquire more money to enjoy their company. Betta attempted several experiments to cure *soro* Ventura's brother. She asked for items of his clothing on which she said several prayers. She enchanted perfumes and prepared several potions, including a piece of flesh from a bat (*noctula*) which were meant to be mixed in Andrea's food.[14] Finally Betta enchanted salt by proferring the following 'moresque' words:

> *melch bumelich, hielachech ixemex, hu inexifech Irrich, tigi mihech Ixibeb, tihabigh idduep*[15]

---

[12] I.M. Lewis, *Ecstatic Religion*, p.79.

[13] B. Malinowski, *Magic, Science and Religion, and Other Essays*, p.71.

[14] AIM Proc Crim. Vol.19B case 46, fols.459, 468, 478-79.

[15] Contemporary Italian translation: *O sale bello/leccato dal sole/ et dessicato dal vento/ che ti raccoglino le belle donne/ e ti cargano le giumente.* (English translation: 'Oh salt, beautiful salt/ the sun licks you up/ and the wind dries you up/ young people gather you/ and mares carry you'.) Ibid., 19B, case 46, fol.477v: 22 August 1600.

Armorial bearings of the Inquisition Tribunal. Originally intended for the Medieval Inquisition, this emblem was adopted by the Roman Inquisition in its fight against the spread of Protestantism.

Chancery of the Inquisitor's Palace, Vittoriosa. Photo – Department of Information.

Plate I

Coat-of-Arms of Pope Gregory XIII (1572-1585). In 1573 Pope Gregory appointed Fra Martino Royas de Portalrubeo as Bishop-Inquisitor of Malta.

Chancery of the Inquisitor's Palace, Vittoriosa. Photo – Department of Information.

Plate II

Portrait of Grand Master Jean Levêque de la Cassiere (1572-1581) by Scipione Pulzone de Gaeta. La Cassiere sought the Vatican's advice over a quarrel that had ensued between him and Bishop Royas.

Sacristy of the Conventual Church of the Order of St John, Valletta.

Plate III

Coat-of-Arms of Mgr Pietro Dusina (1574-1575). Mgr Dusina was sent by Pope Gregory XIII to act as Apostolic Delegate and Inquisitor of the Maltese Islands.

Chancery of the Inquisitor's Palace, Vittoriosa. Photo – Department of Information.

Plate IV

Façade of the Inquisitor's Palace, Vittoriosa. The Inquisitor's Palace had previously served as the Grand Masters' Law Courts. This palace was transformed into the quarters of the Malta Inquisition Tribunal by Mgr Dusina.

Inquisitor's Palace, Vittoriosa. Photo – Noel Buttigieg.

Plate V

Courtyard of the Inquisitor's Palace, Vittoriosa. This courtyard contains 'the oldest ribbed cross-vaults in Malta' (L. Mahoney) – a Gothic roofing technique of the Order's Rhodiote chief engineer Niccolò Flavari.

Inquisitor's Palace, Vittoriosa. Photo – Noel Buttigieg

Plate VI

Coat-of-Arms of Inquisitor Fabio Chigi (1634-1639) later elected Pope Alexander VII (1655-1667).

Chancery of the Inquisitor's Palace, Vittoriosa. Photo – Department of Information.

Plate VII

Coat-of-Arms of Inquisitor Antonio Pignatelli (1646-1649). Like Fabio Chigi, Pignatelli was elected Pope as Innocent XII (1691-1700).

Chancery of the Inquisitor's Palace, Vittoriosa. Photo – Department of Information.

Plate VIII

Coat-of Arms of Inquisitor Federico Borromeo (1653-1655).
Borromeo becme Cardinal of Milan in 1670. Borromeo's relazione
to the Holy See provides valuable information on mid-seventeenth-
century Malta.

Chancery of the Inquisitor's Palace, Vittoriosa. Photo – Department of
Information.

Plate IX

Coat-of-Arms of Inquisitor Leonetto della Corbara (1608-1609). Betta Caloiro died at the Inquisition Prisons during the inquisitorship of Della Corbara. Inquisitor Della Corbara acted against the suggestions of the General Inquisition in Rome.

Chancery of the Inquisitor's Palace, Vittoriosa. Photo – Department of Information.

Plate X

The female prisons at the Inquisitor's Palace, Vittoriosa. Women accused of witchcraft and other offences, usually spent some time in one of the communal cells.

Chancery of the Inquisitor's Palace, Vittoriosa. Photo – Noel Buttigieg.

Plate XI

Aerial view of the Gozo Citadel. The Citadel served as the administrative centre and fortress of Gozo. Because of the very small size of the island, witchcraft and sorcery were a major topic of gossip among its inhabitants.

Photo – Department of Information.

Plate XII

The Sanctuary of Our Lady of Mellieħa. The Augustinian Fra Aurelio Axac used to exorcize people with the blessing of the ecclesiastical authorities at this sanctuary.

Photo – *Tony Terribile.*

Plate XIII

Coat-of-Arms of Inquisitor Raynaldo Corso (1577-1579). Inquisitor Corso was congratulated by the General Inquisition in Rome for having ordered the burning of a number of prohibited books.

Chancery of the Inquisitor's Palace, Vittoriosa. Photo – Department of Information.

Plate XIV

Tombstone of Bishop Tommaso Gargallo (1578-1614). Bishop Gargallo banned all books related to astrology, necromancy, witchcraft and divination, and condemned all those who exercised the magical arts.

Gesù Church, formerly the Jesuits, Valletta.

Plate XV

Coat-of-Arms of Inquisitor Innocenzo del Bufalo (1595-1598).
Inquisitor del Bufalo issued an edict in which he ordered anyone,
who owned and perused prohibited books, to report the matter to
the Holy Office.

Chancery of the Inquisitor's Palace, Vittoriosa. Photo – Department of
Information.

Plate XVI

The use of the term 'enchant', instead of 'treat', sheds light on the view held by the upper clergy that the prayers and invocations recited by healers were in effect spells, and their use of the sign of the cross and the wafer in healing, blasphemous. What they practised was perceived as *magaria* or *fattuchiaria* (*maleficium* or maleficient magic), a form of heresy.

Resort to witchcraft beliefs gained currency when medical knowledge proved inadequate. It usually consisted of a mixture of remedies, based on the accumulated experience of nursing combined to the inherited lore, concerning the healing properties of herbs, accompanied by prayers, charms and spells. In Malta the standard treatment for healing diseases was the 'fumigation' of the patient with burnt ingredients, healing by touch, or by bathing parts of the body.[16] Thus Helena, known as Luna, wife of Pietro Periano of Birkirkara, explained that she could heal the evil eye by washing and fumigating the patient and reciting the Pater Noster, Ave Maria and the Creed, as well as by saying *Giesu autemp trensie per media migliorum Ibat.*[17]

At times she even recited two other spells in Maltese:

Hain chachla hain xehla et hain collia ena nerchiha nachta el heiun men fuchiha elli chenu mia.[18]

and

Chamsa hu chimeisa fuhaijar mimeisa, duheiba mesruga, hu min hainu tichun hainu machirugia.[19]

Having conceded that she had cured many individuals during a span of forty years, Luna recalled a spell which she admitted to have adoperated on Paula, one of her neighbours, some years before the siege of 1565. The spell had originally been taught to her by a woman, since then deceased, known as *Duca* from Birkirkara, who was considered to be a *gran magara* by all the villagers:

---

[16] P. Cassar, 'Healing by sorcery in seventeenth and eighteenth cenury Malta', pp.83-5.

[17] AIM Proc Crim. 20A, case 80, fol.63: 5 April 1602.

[18] English translation: 'Azure eye, (grey) eye/ and Ghajn Kollija/ I loosen it/ and remove (lit.cut off) the evil eyes (from it)/ even if they were a hundred'. Ibid.

[19] English translation: 'Five little five/ small earthen pot and (*mimejsa*)/ and a small gold object (*mesruga*)/ and from his eye may the evil eye be brought out'. Ibid.

Chamar hia chammara tetla men bein le gibel hue tighib ben lachsara mur
ù gibili el chadem bent hattara elli handiha zuemel mitein mur hu gibili el
Hazizi lu chen fein, mur gibihuli fi bebi bexi bel chasap en cassibu.[20]

There is no doubt that prayers of obvious Christian origin were
employed side by side with verses of popular lay origins. The
Church's primary concern centred largely on the misuse of sacraments and sacramentals in attempting to establish contact with the
supernatural through channels other than those accepted by the
Church. Indeed it was not at all rare for members of the clergy to
be accused of such practices under the guise of piety and devotion.
The sacred host, in particular, was perceived as a magical remedy
not only by parishioners, but also by members of the clergy. In 1546
the Dominican prior at Birgu was denounced to the Bishop for
having written the words *Hoc est corpus meum* (This is my body)
on consecrated wafers before communicating the sick.[21] This was a
seemingly common practice, as in 1575 the Apostolic Visitor Mgr
Dusina prohibited the clergy from saying mass over consecrated
wafers upon which prayers and other magical words were
written.[22] Besides, inquisitors frequently admonished people from
lending belief to such practices, but apparently old habits die hard.
In 1625, in an attempt to curb these beliefs, the clergy were obliged
to denounce to the Bishop or the Inquisitor anyone who practiced
magic – a directive that was repeated in 1646.[23]

Catholic Remedies and Healing Rituals

At this point we need to explore those 'remedies' offered by the
Catholic Church and widely used in early modern Malta. The belief
that earthly events could be influenced by supernatural intervention
was not in itself considered to be magical by the Catholic Church.

---

[20] English translation: 'Moon oh moon/ you rise from between the mountains/ and you disappear
between (*lachsara*)/ go and fetch me (*el chadem*) daughter of Hattara/ who has two hundred
horses/ go and fetch me my beloved wherever he is/ go and bring him to my door/ so that I
will hit him (*encassibu*) with canes'. Ibid., fol.64.

[21] Ibid., 1A, case 1: 1 April, 1546.

[22] NLM Libr 643, p.35.

[23] P. Cassar, *Medical History of Malta*, p.426.

The efficacy of prayer as a mechanical means to attain salvation was also widely employed. On its part the Church helped a great deal to weaken the fundamental distinction between prayer and spell.[24] Indeed the Church considered prayer as the most obvious weapon against adversity. It was thus normal for the largely illiterate lay faithful to take up both orthodox and popular attitudes towards prayer and mingle them in a single rite.[25] On its part the Church encouraged prayer of a more orthodox nature, yet the effectiveness of prayers was never put into question, for they continued to form a crucial part of many healing rituals, both in the orthodox form and in the form of *orazioni*. Indeed it was precisely the force attributed to the mere repetition of sacred words that led to abuses. One case study refers to the healing practices of Catherina Borg, an 85 year old widow from Birkirkara, who explained how she adoperated three prayers in Maltese mainly to relieve people from headaches, but she also used the same *incanti* for other diseases.[26] Many a time however Catherina adoperated herbal baths and proferred the *orazione* on a clothing item used by the patient.[27] She even admitted that many women went to her house and asked her to profer some words on their heads in order to heal them from headaches.[28] She even worked out three variations of the same prayer employed to relieve her patients from headaches. In the first prayer she invoked Saint Anne and Saint Philip:

Anna santa Anna santa Maria emdanna san filep ù san gilian farchilelech edach eddeni ù edach edolur elli ma hiepcha ula seha ula nihar[29]

---

[24] K. Thomas, *Religion and the Decline of Magic*, p.46.

[25] J. Skorupski, *Symbol and Theory*, pp.133-34.

[26] *Et questi li dico per guarire diversi morbi come quartana terzana altri febbri e qualsivoglia altro male che vi giuro tutte guariscono.* AIM Proc Crim. 19A, case 31, fol.223v.

[27] Antonina Xeberras of Casal Gadir Bordi brought a skull cap belonging to her five year old girl on which Catherina proferred the oration and performed a herbal bath. Ibid. fol.227v.

[28] Ibid. fols.223: 27 March 1602.

[29] English translation: 'Anne, Saint Anne/ Saint Mary, mother-in-law/ Saint Philip and Saint Julian/ may he cure that malady/ and that woe so it would not last/ neither for an hour nor for a day'. Ibid., fol.223v: Evidence of Catherina Borg given on 27 March 1602.

Accompanied by an Ave Maria, the above oration served to heal the
husband of Imperia Farruge of Tarxien from a choleric disease.[30] In
the second version reference is made to Our Lady, Saint Margaret
and Holy Water:

Acqua benedetta ingenita Indelita esseida santa Maria santa Margarita
hinechulech eddeni ù doluri elli ma hiepichi hula seha ule chin.[31]

In the third form of the same prayer, she invoked Saints Philip and
Julian:

Char verb Inchar San filep San Gilian Hierchi eddeni hue dolur helli ma
hiepichalech hula seha hula nihar.[32]

She was so convinced of the powerful healing effect of the last
oration, that she used it to heal a young man who had turned
dumb.[33]

Catherina was considered to be a great healer so that her
patients hailed from all parts of the island. Her healing method
suggests that 'the successful operation of the magical arts...
depended upon the completion of a formal symbolic exchange.
(while) effective wishes were those that were codified into charms
and incantations'.[34] This may explain why holy men and women
were frequently asked to pray on behalf of a devotee, for they were
presumed to have closer contacts with the sacred and could serve
as mediators.

On its part the Roman Catholic Church tried hard 'to redirect
popular attempts at independent access to the supernatural into

---

[30] Ibid., fol.226: 16 April 1602.

[31] English translation: 'Holy water/ ingenita indelita esseida/ Saint Mary/ and Saint Margaret/
remove for you the malady/ and the woes/ so that it would not last/ neither for an hour nor for
[any] time'. Ibid.

[32] English translation: '(Char verb inchar)/ Saint Philip, Saint Julian/ cures the malady/ and the
woe/ so you would not have it any more/ neither for an hour nor for a day'. Ibid.

[33] ...*circa doi mesi fa essendo venuto da me un giovane che havea perso la parola et era diven-*
tato muto per causa che era andato ad arrobare e fu maltrattato in modo che divento muto e
subito io gli disse questo ultimo incanto et l'ho guarito e subito parlò come era prima. Ibid.

[34] M. Flynn, 'Blasphemy and the play of anger in sixteenth century Spain', p.39.

orthodox channels, thus consolidating its monopoly on dealing with positive and negative supernatural forces alike'.[35]

Exorcism and the Clergy

The Church provided a substantial measure of protection against *maleficium* by exorcism. Exorcism was freely used and generally expected in response to natural threats. Besides the exorcist was frequently called to deal with those affected by madness or alleged demonic possession. Here he was in direct competition with practitioners of popular healing rituals. 'The exorcisms of the Church' also served as 'entirely efficacious remedies for preserving oneself from the injuries of witches' declared H. Kramer and J. Sprenger authors of the *Malleus Maleficarum*. Remedies included holy water, the sign of the cross, blessed candles, ringing of the church bells and readings from the Scriptures.[36]

The repertoire of the sixteenth century exorcist remained as vague as it had been in the Middle Ages when it often involved 'a complex mixture of liturgical and folkloric elements' so that there was no fixed ritual for universal rules.[37] The Franciscan exorcist Fra Girolamo Menghi (1529-1609) considered the orthodox remedies of holy water, pilgrimages, confession, clerical blessings and the sign of the cross as efficacious enough particularly since clerics had the power to bless and heal, with the aid of God and the approval of the Church.[38] Menghi considered these 'ecclesiastical remedies' sufficient to thwart the actions of devils and witches alike.[39] Hence the distinction between official and unofficial exorcists was often ambiguous, at least in terms of the ritual performed.[40]

---

[35] M. O'Neil, "'*Sacerdote ovvero Strione*'", p.53.

[36] K. Thomas, *Religion and the Decline of Magic*, p.588.

[37] R. Kieckhefer, *Magic in the Middle Ages*, p.73.

[38] M. O'Neil, 'Magical healing, love magic and the Inquisition in late sixteenth century Modena', p.91.

[39] Ibid., "'*Sacerdote ovvero Strione*'", p.54.

[40] P. Burke, *The Historical Anthropology of Early Modern Italy*, p.212.

Menghi who wrote 'the classic exorcist manuals of the period' – *Compendio dell'Arte Essorcista* (1576) and the famous *Flagellum Daemonum* (1577) – has been described by D. Gentilcore as 'the exorcist *par excellence* of the latter half of the sixteenth century, writing his manuals from the experience gained while practising in Venice, Bologna and Lombardy'.[41] In a study based on 768 libraries, conducted by G. Romeo, it was found that ninety-two per cent of monasteries and individual ecclesiastics possessing exorcist manuals had at least one of Menghi's books around 1600.[42] Yet Menghi's works were rarely found alongside inquisitorial witchcraft manuals suggesting that his readers, were probably more interested in the practical element of his works than the theoretical. Thus the manuals primarily served as a means of countering the perceived spread of diabolical witchcraft. The manual most often cited in trials involving exorcists is apparently his *Flagellum daemonum*, where it is often mentioned in order to support claims regarding an exorcist's orthodox practice of the art.[43]

That the *Flagellum Daemonum* was consulted in late sixteenth century Malta is confirmed by Fra Aurelio Axac, an Augustinian friar who acted as rector of the Church of Our Lady of Mellieħa. In fact, Axac was one of the few clerics in Malta who had a licence to practice exorcism.[44] In a deposition made to the Inquisitor Innocenzo del Bufalo in 1596, he explained that he read on the head of the 'possessed' and several sick persons. Axac recalled how three years earlier, he had exorcised Imperia widow of Geronimo Bonici of Żabbar. He stated that Imperia used to make sounds similar to those of a bull. His experience in this field helped him diagnose her as *adombrata* (a being with an evil eye). At this point, he asserted to have made use of those exorcisms, found in his copy of the

---

[41] D. Gentilcore, *From Bishop to Witch*, pp. 95, 108.

[42] G. Romeo, *Inquisitori, Esorcisti e Streghe nell'Italia della Controriforma*, pp.122-26.

[43] Ibid., pp.114-16.

[44] On 17 October 1583 Joan Paulo Manduca promised to concede a revenue of six *oncie* from an area of land called *il giardino di Santa Lucia* to the Augustinian friar Aurelio Haxac in order to enable Fra Haxac to set up a friary of his Order at the sanctuary of Our Lady of Mellieha. The friary had to be similar to the one already established in Rome and dedicated to the *Madonna del Populo*. ACM Misc 454, Vol.I pp.83-4.

Flagellum Daemonum, reading them on the patient's head at her house in Żabbar. Axac attributed her sickness to a piece of paper written in Arabic.[45]

The Tridentine Church had managed to control the number of trained licensed exorcists and impose a definite procedure. From the scanty material available in the Inquisition trials, exorcism seem to have been very much in demand since it provides useful insights on the activity of exorcists, extra-canonical and otherwise, in Malta.

One such Inquisition trial, dated 1599, relates how Margarita, wife of Leonardo Psaile of Siġġiewi, was believed to be possessed by an evil spirit. The spirit called *teitihe* had entered Margarita as a result of a spell cast by the negress Joanna at the suggestion of Agatha *figlia di ghergem*. It was alleged that the spell proved successful, since both Joanna and Agatha had promised their soul to the devil.[46] The two exorcists consulted by Margarita – Don Mario Greg parish priest of Lija,[47] and Fra Aurelio Axac, rector of Our Lady of Mellieħa – both agreed that she was possessed by an evil spirit called *teitihe*. Once again Fra Aurelio appears to have been the undisputed expert on the subject and he is reported to have said:

> *dico come pratico di demoniati e spiritati che questa Margarita non è demoniata, ma maleficiata con spirito per via di magarie perche li demoniati non hanno quel intelletto che ha costei ma perdono li sensi, e questa tiene li sensi integri...*[48]

By the turn of the seventeenth century, there appears to have been an upsurge in the number of *spiritati* on the island. In a discussion with Don Angelo Mallia, the tertiary *soro* Margarita, sacristan of the church of Our Lady at Żabbar, expressed her amazement at the fact

---

[45] AIM Proc Crim. 14A, case 13, fols.399-v: 12 January, 1596.

[46] Ibid., 147A, case 77, fol.149-v: 9 August, 1599.

[47] Ibid., fol.148-v.

[48] 'as an expert on the possessed and spirited I confirm that Margarita is not possessed, but bewitched by a spirit due to the intervention of magic because the possessed do not have her kind of intellect but rather they lose their senses, and this one holds her full use of the senses...' Ibid., fols.149-v: 9 August, 1599.

that the number of *spiritati* had greatly increased in the last few years. Don Angelo agreed, stating that in previous years such cases were relatively rare, but that their number had multiplied in recent years. *Soro* Margarita added that Don Michele, parish priest of Burmola, who usually read over the heads of *spiritati*, believed that some appeared to be *spiritati* as their bodies were invaded by the souls of those who die an evil death. At this point Don Angelo felt the need to correct *soro* Margarita by asserting that according to the teachings of the Church those who die could only go to heaven, hell or purgatory.[49]

Don Michele's case provides evidence that ordinary clerics frequently succumbed to pressures in attempting to heal, or actively took the situation into their hands. Incidentally such popular beliefs remained strongly entrenched in popular culture, so much so that they were even recorded by the nineteenth century Sicilian ethnographer G. Pitrè.[50] The popular reaction changed little, but continued to see the devil's work in every malady.

Popular Perception and the Cult of Saints

Reaction to malady and misfortune consequently often entailed some recourse to the saints. The wise woman frequently accompanied her cures with invocations (*orazioni*) to a saint, one specifically related to the ailment by a detail or characteristic mentioned in his or her *historiola*. Society could also invoke the power of the sacred through the saints of the Catholic Church by means as diverse as prayer, pilgrimage and relic-veneration. The increasing demands of this Christian society for access to sacred power possessed by saints were intended to counter natural misfortunes and calamities. All these manifestations in some way expressed the meaning and role of sanctity in early modern society.

---

[49] Ibid., 22C, case 237, fol.962: 27 August, 1604.

[50] *'La pazzia è effetto di spiriti maligni che invadono il disgraziato infermo... che il povero pazzo sia un individuo invaso dagli spiriti maligni è vecchia superstizione nel nostro popolino. Le donniciuole, specialmente credono che la pazzia consista in uno di questi spiriti, il quale si permette di prendere alloggio dentro il corpo di un individuo e non ne vuole più uscire'*. G. Pitrè, *Medicina Popolare Siciliana*, pp.393-94.

Saints had come to represent 'the sacred' in an accessible form, independent of any clerical intervention. The saint belongs to and reflects the society which produce and honour him. Therefore he represents the sacred, where the sacred meant power – without limitations or restrictions – over the natural order of things.[51] This explains why P. Camporesi described the saint as a 'magician-cum-prophet who has succeeded in mastering the occult world, in reading the future, in penetrating the most jealously guarded secrets of the present'. The saint is the one 'who overturns physical laws, who reveals the unexpected, who prophesies a change of state, who inhabits another dimension full of remarkable, unheard-of and spectacular phenomena'.[52] Similarly the eminent anthropologist Malinowski, asserts that saints become, in popular practice, passive accomplices of magic. Thus they can provide rain by being placed in a field, stop flows of lava by confronting them, halt the progress of a disease, of a blight or of a plague of insects.[53]

The brief magical formula that followed the *historiola* – the brief narration of an episode in the life of Christ, or Our Lady or any saint, recited as part of a healing ritual – was usually pronounced *sotto voce*, its very secrecy giving it limitless power. By their nature, such words had to escape the comprehension of the uninitiated in order to be effective. G. Cocchiara identifies this part of the invocation as a survival of pre-Christian magical formula on to which has been tacked the Christian *historiola*.[54] Yet often the magical formula itself, which depended on the exorcising power of words, took on a Christian form, as in the case of a cure which the eighty-year-old Betta Caloiro acknowledged to have learned from her deceased brother Bernardo.

This particular *historiola* is revealing, since it is garbed in a mixture of Italian, Castilian and Latin words – languages that were definitely widely practised in the Three Cities of Birgu, Burmola and Senglea under the Order. The very restricted urban

---

[51] D. Gentilcore, *From Bishop to Witch*, pp.167-68.

[52] P. Camporesi, *The Incorruptible Flesh*, p.36.

[53] B. Malinowski, 'The role of magic and religion', p.40.

[54] G. Cocchiara, *Il Linguaggio della Poesia Popolare*, pp.123-26.

space available – before the building of Valletta in 1566 – ensured
that the Maltese population living there could certainly pick up a
large number of foreign words from the heterogeneous community
in the area, and this word-mixture was used profusely even by
locals. Betta herself had asserted, in one of her depositions, that
her family hailed from Burmola, and precisely from the Santa
Helena area.[55]

*Virgo gloriosa tam formosa come la rosa dioscherio nascer alas terras por
esser vinno l'angelo san Gabriel pregonto su pastora havia bon dia un
figlio parco Maria con tanta allegria todo il mondo salvaria sino il perro
nol giudio, mi segnor giesu Christo meso nelles manos los clavaros la
corona l'espinaro et spersio sangue laltra chittaros Santa Maria la
limpiada, Santa Maria non fagas esto sin con sogno sin con flava havemo
da passar, passamo di Christo andar, veni San Martin con gran dolor
partio lo manto de color medio su Signor medio su peccador, Povera vita
tu via gadagnas romeria ij trido Inventada ij trido illechiada sina il ferta
del paradiso, sin il ferta del Inferno ressuretione vita eternam amen.*[56]

Betta also proferred the following invocation:

*verbo ti voglio dire verbo de nostro Signore miso In ligno della croce per
noi peccatori contanta bella braccio In celo l altro Interra quanto dirò
Aglio chi dici fo di grendi Il perinuri triniati nesci di xiuri picculi e grandi
trenta tre anni trasi ciaghi frischi e novi maiestati Santo Pietro responde
San Gioanni beata Maria suo verbo so In vizza quattro volti vi la morte,
resurettione vita eternam amen.*[57]

But Betta Caloiro admitted that she did not know the meaning of
the words. She added that the invocation was taught to her by Don
Francesco Habela, who read it from a book when she was still six
years old. Don Habela, Betta explained, lived in a house at the
Burmola garden near the church of St Margaret.[58] From Betta's

---

[55] AIM Proc Crim. 19B, case 46, fols.477Av-478: 22 August 1600.

[56] Ibid., fol.460v: 14 October 1599. This *historiola* must be understood within the political situation of the central Mediterranean during the three decades preceeding the siege of 1565. The
relatively long reign of the Castilian Grand Master Juan D'Homedes between 1536-1553,
coupled with the dominant position of Spain at the time, meant almost total Spanish domina-
tion of the area.

[57] Ibid., 19B, case 46, fol.463: 25 April, 1599.

[58] Don Habela was an uncle of Magnifico Alessandro Habela and an ancestor of Giovanni
Francesco Habela, Vice-Chancellor of the Order of St John and author of *Della Descrittione
di Malta* – the first Maltese history book published in Malta in 1647. Ibid., fol.465.

deposition we learn that medical knowledge often proved inadequate, while magic was always put forward as a substitute. Thus Betta explained how she became acquainted with magical healings. At the age of six, she had been bewitched by a woman of the village and her nose became distorted. Betta spent the next twenty-five years visiting several physicians who could not offer any remedy. Finally a doctor from Licata, who lived in Fort St Angelo during the reign of Grand Master D'Homedes, was able to cure her by using a mixture that included lead. She thus used lead to cure others.[59] In her deposition of 25 April 1600 Betta declared:

> I heard that such remedies function through the intervention of Christ, and saints Cosmas and Damian, physicians of Christ thanks to the Our Father and Hail Mary which I proferred, as well as the burning of blessed incense and myrrh which was an ointment of Christ. The remedy even served as medicine.[60]

Betta's deposition provides a valuable insight into the practising of magic remedies during the early years of the Order's rule when popular attempts at independent access to the supernatural were either tolerated or ignored by church authorities. Thus Betta recalled how on the eve of St John the Baptist (23 June), she used to meet other girls of her age at the house of a Sicilian woman called Victoria, sited in the Birgu marina. Victoria used to teach the girls the recitation of a number of invocations.[61] Betta added that she had been taught a large number of invocations in her youth, but she had forgotten most of them in her old age. When asked why she adoperated such invocations, she expressed surprise, retorting that blessed medicine heals better as it possessed more virtue.[62]

From Betta's deposition, it transpires that both the medical doctor from Licata and Don Francesco Habela approved such remedies. It may appear a little strange to us that the culture of the

---

[59] According to Betta the physician had apparently escaped from Licata when the city was stormed by the Turks. Ibid.

[60] Ibid., fol.465.

[61] Ibid., fol.482: 30 August, 1600.

[62] Ibid., fol.464-v.

'learned' élite was not maintained completely distinct from popular culture. In an attempt to analyse this phenomenon, P. Burke points out that:

> The élites of Europe at this period might reasonably be described as 'bi-cultural'. They had access to culture which the ordinary people did not share... On the other hand, they participated in popular culture... If they had not done so, they would have found it difficult to communicate with their wives and daughters, who were generally excluded from the high culture of the time.[63]

Historiolas and Magical Cures

The cures proferred were quite varied, tending to follow very similar patterns. Two *historiolas* on healing, learned in Naples and prac-tised in Malta – one for a specific malady and another for general needs – are recorded to have been adoperated by Andrella Rispulo, wife of the deceased padron Bernardo.[64] Andrella, of Neapolitan origins, explained how she had learned two *incanti* for the healing of the spleen and women's breasts while in Naples eighteen years before. She admitted to have adoperated the *incanti* on several occasions and explained how she prepared them at sunset by filling a bowl with water and then recited a *Pater Noster* and *Ave Maria* and inserting a string, a needle and a comb in the water while reciting the following words:[65]

Madonna Santa Maria alla via s'andava scontransi una poverella che forte si lamentava, ci disse nostra Donna che hai che tanto forte vi lamentati Issa ci disse m'è venuto lu lippo alla ciccina non posso allactare ne a me ne a miei vicini, dice nostra donna piglia l'aco e lo pettine de la capo e mettiti a

---

[63] P. Burke, *Venice and Amsterdam*, pp.xix-xx.

[64] The Neapolitan Rispolo brothers – Bernardino and Santillo – migrated to Malta prior to the siege of 1565 settling down as *padroni* of corsair vessels in Senglea. They were a leading entrepreneurial family of the Harbour area who symbolized success in Maltese commercial activity at the time. See: C. Cassar, 'Economy, society and identity in early modern Malta', ch.4.

[65] AIM Proc Crim. 20A, case 95. fols 375-v: 6 January 1602.

cantari li santi ciaghi di Christo cosi non argo et moglia nonnullo mali non
ci si accogli con quella, Santo Petro la ditto, Santo Nicola l'ha benedittu ne
pungiri ne fare male possa ne a vui ne a lu christianu.[66]

Apparently Neapolitan women had more faith in the cures provided
by old women and expert matrons than those of the physicians, but
by the last decades of the sixteenth century even the Church in
Naples had began to control the spread of such practices.[67]

Andrella also recited another *historiola* for the healing of the
spleen in which Our Lady, and saints Peter and Nicholas are similarly invoked:

Madonna Santa Maria per la via s'andava ci scontrau un poverellu che forti
si lamentava, dici che hai poverellu che gran lamenti fai, ci dice piglia novi
chiuppi di canna e mettili a pirciari, e come li chiaghi di Christo non arsiro
ne doglia cosi non arda ne manco ci doglia e nullo mali si ci accoglia San
Petro, l'ha ditto Santo Nicola l'Ha benedetto, Santo Nicola d'avaro non
piangiri possu ne fare mali ne aissu ne à nissuno christiano.[68]

Andrella believed that it was in virtue of the sacred words hailing
Christ, the Virgin and the saints that she was able to heal the
diseases; but she promised Inquisitor Verallo to stop making use of
these healing orations.[69]

Although the first *historiola* was meant for general needs and the
other for a specific malady, they both follow a similar format,
namely that of a healing invocation. These invocations became

---

[66] Our Lady, Saint Mary on her way she went and met a poor girl who complained bitterly, and
Our Lady asked her, 'What do you have that you are complaining so bitterly?' The girl told
her, 'I cannot lactate neither to my child nor to those of my neighbours'. Our Lady advised her,
'Pick a hair pin and a comb from your head and start singing about the holy wounds of Christ
so that you won't hurt and suffer no harm.' This has been stated by St Peter and blessed by St
Nicholas and it could neither prick nor hurt you nor any other Christian. Ibid, fol.375.

[67] G. Romeo, *Inquisitori, Esorcisti e Streghe nell'Italia della Controriforma*, pp.204, 220.

[68] Our Lady, Saint Mary on her way she went and met a poor boy who complained bitterly, and
Our Lady asked him, 'What do you have that you are complaining so bitterly?' Our Lady
advised him, 'Pick up nine cane sticks and pierce them, and as the holy wounds of Christ did
not hurt nor harm so your disease will not make you suffer nor harm you.' This has been stated
by St Peter and blessed by St Nicholas and it could neither make you cry nor hurt you nor any
other Christian. AIM Proc Crim. 20A, case 95, fol.375v.

[69] Ibid. fol.376.

effective as the healer exorcised or cast the malady out of the body, by reciting an *historiola*, which told of a brief episode in the life of Jesus, the Virgin or the saints, and wherein a disease was often specified. The *historiola* operated on the principle of analogy. Hence illnesses were often sampled with the names of saints, who were in turn invoked by the people as thaumaturgical healers.

Among her many healing and magical activities, Betta Caloiro explained how she taught a *historiola* in honour of St Anastasia for the healing of headaches:

> *Santa Anastasia in mezzo della porta sedia passau Christo ci disse che hai, la mia testa mi dole veni qui t'imparo l'oratione, va a Santo Antonio levami dalla testa questi dolori.*[70]

Similarly the notorious witch Luna Periano of Birkirkara taught a *historiola* for the healing of the eyes:

> *passau la vergine Maria per andare via sentau sopra la pietra de marmaria passò Il Sig.r Iddio trovò la madre con la mano al ochio ci disse che hai nel ochio gli respose l'ochio me dole, gli disse andate nel Gorto fatto da man mia cogliete un finochieto e con quello linite detto ochio.*[71]

This and other popular healing rituals described above are evidence that the Christian element and influence were almost always present in *historiolas*. Indeed the pious sentiments expressed in such invocations, the appeal to the saints, and the use of masses, the lighting of candles or lamps, and the orthodox prayers which accompany such rituals, indicate that these remedies developed largely as extensions of ecclesiastical ritual remedies, and not simply from some pre-Christian source.[72]

---

[70] While St Anastasia was sitting on her doorstep, Christ passed by and asked her 'What do you have?' 'My head is hurting me.' 'Come here I will teach you an oration; go to St Anthony and say 'Take these pains from my head'. Ibid., 19B, case 46, fol. 460: 14 October, 1599.

[71] On her way the Virgin Mary sat on the rock of marmaria. The Lord God passed by and found his mother holding her eye and he asked her why. She said 'my eye is hurting me', and he told her, 'go to the orchard which I have set up and pick a fennel with which to rub your eye. AIM Proc Crim. 20A, case 80, fol.63v: 5 April, 1602.

[72] M. O'Neil, 'Magical healing, love magic and the Inquisition in late sixteenth century Modena', p.91.

When Don Antonio Bartolo learned of the practice of the cult of St Domenica, among several Mosta women, he immediately denounced the matter to the Inquisition and condemned these practices as *superstitiose da falsa religione benche da donna devote* (superstitious practices of a false religion though performed by devout women). Don Bartolo provided some details on the celebration of the ceremony. He asserted that amongst others, these women light candles every Saturday for thirteen consecutive weeks and on each occasion they always light a new candle and recite several orations. After the thirteenth Saturday, the women pick up all the remains of the candles and they ask a priest to celebrate mass in honour of Saint Domenica. Don Bartolo asserted that he checked in the catalogue of saints for the name of Saint Domenica but could not find it anywhere, though she appears to have been venerated in the Gallican rite and recalled how a chapel was dedicated to her at Żurrieq.[73]

The preoccupation of Don Antonio Bartolo is an indication that the post-Tridentine Catholic Church felt the need to respond to the 'ignorance and superstition' of the faithful with a mixture of cathechesis and repression. In the wake of Trent, such practices were frequently condemned. Hence both secular and Church courts participated in an intense effort to upgrade the religious practices and moral values of society by enforcing stricter and orthodox standards of belief and behaviour. Such a view seems to concur with the suggestion put forward by M. O'Neil that exorcisms have helped in more than one way to control the spread of a 'witch panic' similar to the ones that characterized contemporary northern Europe.[74]

As always, popular medicine continued to be a predominantly female field, in part because poor, elderly women were frequently driven to the margins of society and so also depended on such services for their livelihood, their activities often taking on an

---

[73] There was yet another chapel dedicated to St Domenica in Żabbar. AIM Proc Crim. 23A, case 317, fol.309-v: 6 December 1604.

[74] M. O'Neil, "'Saccerdote ovvero Strione'", p.81 n.42.

aspect of disguised begging. Yet healing and health were also a natural part of the female domain in early modern Malta: part of the woman's concern for the family's survival and well-being. Wise women – like the saints who cured diseases – continued to fulfill an ambivalent but necessary role in society. A precise causal agent (as far as the patient-victim was concerned) also meant the imminent potentiality of the cure. In the way that the magical representation of illness was mixed with the feeling of being dominated by dark forces, so the magical representation of the cure was mixed with the feeling of being cured.[75] Finally, one should not underestimate the importance of the healing rituals in the 'acting out of sickness, and the symbolic treatment of disease in its social context', which must have appealed to the mind and imagination of the client.[76]

---

[75] E. De Martino, *Sud e Magia*, p.21.

[76] K. Thomas, *Religion and the Decline of Magic*, p.245.

Necromancy and Learned Magic

In practice, the Church tended to dump all 'superstitious magic' together, believing that whatever the purpose, the means were more or less the same. Rituals as diverse as healing, divination, love magic, maleficient spells and treasure hunting (a branch of learned or élite magic) tended to be condemned together, because of the belief that they all acquired their potency through the devil.[1]

Yet each type was used under widely different circumstances and frequently performed by separate practitioners. Healing rituals, served a purpose which at first glance is quite distinct from that of divination or love magic. Despite differences in intent, all these forms – even the most maleficient – sought to bring about some sort of order to the profane world by tapping the sacred. So it is no accident that they would overlap one another. Here we will try to explore the relationships between the various types of magic, whether they were presumed to derive their power from God and even the saints, that is the divine, or from demons, spirits and from Satan himself – the diabolical face of the sacred – in a persistent attempt to control daily events.

---

[1] P. Burke asserts that 'the distinction between magic and witchcraft was not a sharp one. There was a cluster of terms in Italian which might be translated 'magician': *mago, nigromante, incantator* (feminine *incantatrice*), or *sortilego*. These terms referred to people whose use of rituals and spells gave them supernatural powers which they might use for good or evil'. P. Burke, 'Witchcraft and magic in Renaissance Italy', p.34.

Occult Philosophy in the Renaissance

The Holy Office treated learned magic as the principal threat, in part because it purported to offer an alternative cosmology, whereas popular magic tended toward the particular and the defensive, without the cloak of an explicit doctrine. Of course, it possessed an implicit cosmology and sense of the divine, one that was transmitted rather than taught; but it was the sub-system of the necromancer, with its circulating, secret texts, which became of greater concern to the Church after Trent. Thus although popular magic sought recourse to the omnipotent in both its divine and diabolical forms, it worked alongside Catholic rituals intended to procure protection and security during moments of crisis, not at tempting an all-inclusive interpretation of reality. Even though popular and learned magic were denounced together and with equal vehemence by the Church, learned magic was potentially considered to be the more dangerous. It is essential at this point to give a general view of the emergence of learned magic and what it sought to achieve.

The 'occult philosophy' of the Renaissance was compounded of Hermeticism, as revived by Marsilio Ficino (1433-99), to which in Florence, Pico della Mirandola (1463-94) added a Christian version of the Jewish Cabala. The Cabalist side is fundamental because it exercised a most powerful influence on the history of religion. The word Cabal means 'tradition'. It was believed that when God gave the Law to Moses, he also gave a second revelation regarding the secret meaning of Law. This esoteric tradition was said to have been transmitted down the ages orally by initiates. It was a mystic cult rooted in the Scriptures, serving basically as a method of religious contemplation which could easily evolve into some sort of religious magic.[2]

The presence of Cabala in the Christian tradition owes its origins to the Catalan philospher and mystic Ramon Lull (1232-1316). During the High Middle Ages, the Iberian peninsula was a centre for the three great monotheistic religions of the Mediterranean: Judaism, Christianity, and Islam. Christianity and the Catholic

---

[2] F. Yates, *The Occult Philosophy*, p.2.

Church were dominant, but a large part of the peninsula was still under Muslim rule. Spain was also the centre for the strongest Jewish community of the time. Lull, a devout Christian Catholic, learned much from the brilliant civilization of the Spanish Muslims, with its mysticism, philosophy, art, science and cultural achievements. He was even well acquainted with the cultural achievements that the Sephardic Jews had intensively developed; especially their medicine, philosophy and their mysticism, better known as the Cabala. Lull tried to define the basic principles of all three religious traditions to bind all three together in a common philosophical, scientific, and mystic basis.[3]

The scientific principles, held in common by Christians, Muslims and Jews, on which Lull based his Art, was the theory of elements assuming that everything in the natural world is composed of four elements: earth, water, air, fire. To these correspond the elemental qualities: cold, moist, dry, hot – which, when mixed together, could be exactly classified and graded. The elemental theory had its prolongation in the stars since the planets and signs of the zodiac exert predominantly cold, moist, dry, or hot influences. The elemental theory – which was originally elaborated by the Greek philosopher Empedocles in the fifth century BC – derived its teachings from astrology.[4] Lull fused the Jewish Cabala with astrology. Lull's new approach was to have profound influence throughout Europe for centuries and he can easily be considered as the precursor of the scientific method. The great figures of Renaissance Neoplatonism came to include Lull in their interests.

The Christian Cabala was formulated by Pico della Mirandola in Florence, shortly before the expulsion of the Jews from the Spanish domains in 1492. He learnt the techniques from Spanish Jews, but interpreted them in a Christian direction. Pico associated Cabala with Hermeticism by introducing Hermetic magic into the system. In turn Cabala played a fundamental role in the so-called Neoplatonism of the Renaissance, the movement inaugurated in Florence by Marsilio

---

[3] Ibid., p.9.

[4] Ibid., p.10.

Ficino and Pico della Mirandola in the late fifteenth century. The Cabalist side lent powerful support to the whole movement, particularly thanks to the revelation of new spiritual depths in the Scriptures.

Neoplatonism was a rich amalgam of genuinely platonic teachings and Late Antiquity philosophical occultisms. Prominent among the texts of this type which attracted Pico and Ficino was the *Corpus Hermeticum*, supposedly written by Hermes Trismegistus, a mythical Egyptian sage who was believed to have lived at about the same time as Moses and came to represent ancient wisdom – the remote source of Plato himself.[5] Into this atmosphere of Neoplatonism, with its Hermetic tradition, it did not prove difficult to assimilate the Cabala, which was believed to be the ancient wisdom tradition descended from Moses.

Pico's account of Cabala is contained in the seventy-two Cabalist *Conclusions* which in his opinion went to confirm the Christian religion from its Judaistic foundations. Pico considers the *ars combinandi*, which expounds the theories of the thirteenth-century Sephardic-Jewish mystic Abraham Abulafia, as somewhat similar to the Art of Ramon Lull.[6] He thus recognized Lull as a Cabalist. Since the Cabala confirms the truth of Christianity, for Pico and his followers, Cabalist methods and techniques of religious meditation could be adopted by Christians.[7]

Probably through the influence of exiled Spanish Jews, interest in Cabala increased enormously by the end of the fifteenth century and throughout the sixteenth century. In Italy, the Cabala was fervently taken up by several enthusiasts for Catholic reform.

One of the most influential Cabalists in Italy, Francesco Giorgi (1466-1540), was a Franciscan friar, 'imbued with Renaissance Neoplatonism and all its Hermetic adjuncts, and above all with Christian Cabala, re-inforced by Franciscan myticism'.[8] The French translation of Giorgi's work, better known as *L'Harmonie du Monde* by Guy Le

---

[5] D.P. Walker, *Spiritual and Demonic Magic from Ficino to Campanella*, esp. pp.40-43, 64-72; F. Yates, *Giordano Bruno and the Hermetic Tradition*, chs.1-4.

[6] F. Yates, ibid., p.96.

[7] Ibid., *The Occult Philosophy*, pp.17-22.

[8] F. Yates, Ibid., pp.29-36.

Fèvre de la Boderie in 1578, contributed notably to an intensification of interest in Giorgi. According to F. Yates, the prefaces by La Boderie and his brothers are a reflection of the Giorgi revival in the late French Renaissance, 'a time when interest in the Christian Cabala seems to have increased'. This is because:

> the readers of the French translation are told of the numerological and architectural formulations of universal harmony... (while) the importance of the temple of Solomon as the great exemplar of architectural numerology is emphasized. The preface is a remarkable statement of Neoplatonic philosophy which emphasises the Cabalist, Hermetic and Pythagorean interpretations of the movement. Above all, the La Boderie prefaces emphasize the Christian application of the Cabala.[9]

These influences were taken over wholeheartedly in the Neoplatonist theories of the time, including the whole tradition of Pythagoro-Platonic numerology, of world and human harmony, as well as the Vitruvian theory of architecture, which for Giorgi had a religious significance to be connected with the Temple of Solomon.[10] This ultimate link with the Temple of Solomon was a widely held theory throughout the Renaissance.[11]

In the French Renaissance, the influence of Giorgi was so strong that it became one of the channels through which Hermetic and Cabalist influences flowed into thinking, art, science and literature. Giorgi's presentation of universal harmony influenced the theories of the Academy of Poetry and Music.[12] 'Public' lessons in necromancy seem to have been the order of the day in France during the sixteenth century. Thus we find that in 1596 Tiberio Camarda, an inhabitant of Malta, asserted to the Inquisition that his father – by then eighty years old – had been instructed in necromancy while living in France.[13]

Giorgi may seem very different from his contemporary, Henry Cornelius Agrippa (1486-1535) – who laid great emphasis on the

---

[9] Ibid., p.65.

[10] D.P. Walker, *Spiritual and Demonic Magic*, pp.112-19.

[11] R. Taylot, 'Architecture and magic', pp.131-403.

[12] F. Yates, *The French Academies of the Sixteenth Century*, passim.

[13] AIM Proc Crim. 15B, case 111, fol.666v: 16 October, 1596.

magical aspect – but the angelic thought-structure within which
Agrippa operates is really the same as that supported by Giorgi.
Like Giorgi, Agrippa concentrates on numbers, and on proportions
in man and the universe. Agrippa may be called a Renaissance Neoplatonist and a Christian Cabalist, deeply interested in religious
reform. The outlook of the *De Occulta Philosophia* is almost iden-
tical to that pro-pounded by Giorgi in the *De Harmonia Mundi*. But
he tends to rely more on magical advice than Giorgi, so that in the
late sixteenth century, Agrippa gained the reputation of the
Archmagus. The eventual transformation of Agrippa as the personification of evil sorcery seems to have been finally achieved by the
Jesuit, Martin del Rio, in his authoritative work on magic,
Disquisitionum Magicarum, libri sex, first published in Louvain
around 1599.[14] As a result, Agrippa became the scapegoat of the
whole movement, and was hounded as a black magician.[15]

The image on man as sorcerer which emerges from the hermetic
writings fitted in well with humanist ideas about the dignity of
man. This seems to have elevated the status of the magician during
the fifteenth and sixteenth centuries, just as there was a rise in
status of the artist. Magic did not merely survive into this period; it
was revived. In any case, it is impossible to draw a sharp distinction
between 'reactionary' magic and 'progressive' science.[16] This
explains why in the opinion of F. Yates, in the opening years of the
seventeenth century,

> every kind of magic and occultism was rampant... There can be little doubt
> that the esoteric and demon-ridden atmosphere of this period was the final
> outcome – as it were, the decadence – of the revaluation of magic ulti-
> mately deriving from Ficino and Pico and which, extravagantly continued
> by such descendants of theirs as Cornelius Agrippa, had received support
> from the animistic interpretations of nature of the Renaissance philo-
> sophers.[17]

---

[14] C.G. Nauert, *Agrippa and the Crisis of Renaissance Thought*, p.328.

[15] F. Yates, *The Occult Philosophy*, pp.37-47.

[16] P. Burke, 'Witchcraft and magic in Renaissance Italy: Gian Francesco Pico and his *Strix*', p.33.

[17] F. Yates, *Giordano Bruno and the Hermetic Tradition*, p.433.

Prohibited Literature and the Maltese Élite

In an age, where everything was believed to work by hand, stars and machines alike, it was not possible to explain any phenomenon without bringing in the intervention of the Devil. Otherwise, points out L. Febvre, how are we to explain the fact that, with all his great intellect, and his boldness in matters of religion, Jean Bodin – one of the great minds of the late sixteenth century – came to publish one of the most depressing works of the age, the *Traité de la Démonomanie des Sorciers* (1580) which had countless editions. Devils were everywhere. They haunted the most intelligent minds of the age as well as the common folk.[18] In this respect, the illiterate and literate worlds were much closer to each other, since books contained a series of prescriptions and formulae that used divine or angelic names to counteract all bodily ills.[19]

There was a constant interaction between oral/popular culture and learned/élite culture, if such clear-cut distinctions can be applied to social life in early modern Europe. Mary O'Neil demonstrates that, in sixteenth century northern Italy, priests were caught in an ambivalent cultural situation. Ideally they 'should have constituted the primary barrier against rustic error', yet the line between 'popular demands and the requirements of orthodoxy' was rather nebulous.[20]

The Maltese Church was likewise influenced and conditioned by the demands and practices of the faithful. The clergy were potential mediators in this regard too. Reference to the popularity of such usages is made in a case involving two thirty-two year-old priests, who in 1647 confessed to Inquisitor Pignatelli (later Pope Innocent XII) that, at the age of sixteen, they had practised some experiments about which they had read in a manuscript. Among other recipes, they could recall that this book included formulae to attain

---

[18] L. Febvre, 'Witchcraft: nonsense or a mental revolution?', p.189.

[19] E.M. Butler, *Ritual Magic*, p.32.

[20] M. O'Neil, "*Sacerdote Ovvero Strione*". Ecclesiastical and superstitious remedies in 16th century Italy', p.75.

immunity against fire-arms, as well as others on love magic. They even tried some love magic experiments.[21]

The possession of such literature was prohibited by both the Church and the State. In a manuscript entitled *Pratica per Procedere Nelle Cause del Sant'Officio*, chapters eleven and fourteen condemned books on geomancy, hydromancy, aeromancy, pyromancy, onomancy, necromancy, the magic arts, sorcery, prophecy, divination, auguries and related enchantments. Chapter eleven, which gives a detailed account of what is meant by sorcery, specifies that sorcery could be practised after having consulted various books and writings.[22] The Inquisitor therefore had to make sure that a perquisition of the belongings of the accused sorcerer should take place. There follows a list of items which were ordinarily used in such experiments: inscribed characters, magical experiments, 'virgin' paper and books like the *Key of Solomon*, the *Alma di Centum Regum*, *Arta Notoria*, *Paolina*, *Cornelio Agrippa*, *Pietro d'Albano*, *Opus Mathematicum*, magical instruments such as swords, mirrors, rings, rods, magnets and the like that the Inquisition was also advised to confiscate forthwith.[23]

Paul IV's Index – printed and promulgated in Rome in 1559 – condemned the *opera omnia* of about five hundred and fifty authors, as well as many individual titles. P.F. Grendler calls it 'the first (index) to manifest the puritan characteristic of Counter Reformation censorship, with the result that it vastly enlarged prohibitions in the field of vernacular literature'.[24] This Index was much larger than its predecessors and included some new categories of prohibitions. It significantly condemned nearly sixty editions of the Bible, while banning the printing and possession of Bibles in

---

[21] AIM Proc Crim. 61A, case 45, fol.219: 11 March 1647. C. Cassar, 'Witchcraft beliefs and social control', p.324. A. Bonnici discusses the case in his, *Il-Maltin u l-Inkizizzjoni f'Nofs is-Seklu Sbatax*, p.118, but misguidedly, Bonnici refers to the two young priests as two young men.

[22] AIM Misc. 2, ch. 11, pp.31-42.

[23] AIM Misc.2, ch.11, p.34.

[24] P.F. Grendler, *The Roman Inquisition*   *...netian Press*: 1540-1605, p.116.

any vernacular except with the permission of the Inquisition.[25] Newly prohibited were a number of works of vernacular literature that were judged to be anticlerical, immoral, lascivious or obscene. These in cluded works by Aretino, Machiavelli, Boccaccio and Rabelais.[26] All anonymous works published in the early part of the century were banned, as were all books on magic and necromancy while some famous occult books, like Agrippa, were banned outright. Rule IX of the Tridentine Index prohibited all other occult titles, except astrological works that preserved free will.[27] It went on to forbid the acquisition, owning, reading and study, as well as dealing in books or printed matter containing orations, incantations, stories, predictions for the year and prognostications.[28]

Yet occult titles surfaced regularly in the Inquisition trials of those who pursued the hidden arts. Notary Jacobo Baldacchino, a close friend of Mastro Andrea Axac – a condemned heretic – was accused of keeping such prohibited literature at home. In the sentence pronounced against him on 19 September 1574, there is reference to his personal collection of books on necromancy which included the *Centum Regnum, La Clavicola di Solomone (Key of Solomon), Il Ragiel, Il Libro delli Esperimenti di Cornelio Agrippa, Li Prestigii, La Compositione di Quattro Anelli, 'et molti esperimenti di questa maledetta arte'.*[29]

Cornelius Agrippa's *De Occulta Philosophia,* the most popular book of magic in the Kingdom of Naples, was banned by the ecclesiastical authorities, who kept a vigilant eye on the activities of booksellers, often resorting to subterfuge to catch sly merchants in the act.[30] Johann Weyer, in his *De Praestigiis Daemonum,* first edited in 1563, dared to suggest that witches were not infernal agents, but merely silly and deluded old women, suffering from

---

[25] Ibid., p.117.

[26] See Appendix: List of Books burned by the Inquisition at Vittoriosa in 1609.

[27] P.F. Grendler, ibid., p.196.

[28] AIM Misc.2, ch.14, p.45.

[29] AIM Proc Crim. 2B, case 31, fol.338v.

[30] P. Lopez, *Inquisizione, Stampa e Censura nel Regno di Napoli Tra '500 e '600,* p.181.

melancholy.[31] Perhaps Weyer's book was condemned because he
was a disciple of Agrippa who minimizes the evil role of witches.
Whatever the case Weyer's book was put on the Index even though
his belief seems to have been taken up by several prelates like the
Inquisitor of Malta, later Cardinal, Federico Borromeo (1653-1655). In
his report to the Holy See, Borromeo asserted that magical practices
exerted direct influence only on weaker members of Maltese
society, especially women and 'simpletons'.[32]

Works like *La Clavicola di Solomone* (*The Key of Solomon*) often
'circulated clandestinely in jealously-guarded hand-written versions,
not primarily because of the difficulty of obtaining printed copies or
the fear of prosecution, but because printed texts were considered
useless'.[33] The book had to be copied out by the magician himself,
using a consecrated pen and paper, preferably from a well-known
magician's copy.[34] Such texts and loose sheets were usually hidden
by the magician among other sheets and papers to avoid discovery.
As a complete guide to magic, as well as the art of medicine, *The
Key of Solomon* was considered worth the great effort and expense
required to track down and obtain a copy. This explains why Dr
Galeazzo Cademusto went to the length of writing a book on necromancy in his own handwriting. This book was obtained by a
grammar school teacher, Dr Alfonso di Thomaso, a Neapolitan, who
on being sentenced to row on the galleys, passed it on to his pupil
Alessandro Faiensa, brother-in-law of the lawyer Dr Joanne
Calli.[35]

One would note that with the mission of Mgr Dusina in Malta,
the arm of the Inquisition grew so powerful that when the
Guardiano del Porto allowed Mastro Giovanni Barbiere to import
from Palermo books for Maltese friaries, he was promptly put

---

[31] H. Trevor-Roper, *Religion, the Reformation and Social Change*, p.146; C. Baxter, 'Johann
Weyer's *De Praestigiis Daemonum*: Unsystematic psychpathology', pp.53-75.

[32] NLM Libr. 23, p.258; *Malta Letteraria*, II (1927), p.189.

[33] D. Gentilcore, *From Bishop to Witch*, p.229.

[34] E.M. Butler, *Ritual Magic*, p.48.

[35] AIM Proc Crim. 6C, fol.1037: 2 November 1582. witness of Dr Joanne Calli.

under accusation and a case opened against him.[36] We learn that on 13 September 1577, Inquisitor Raynaldo Corso was congratulated by the General Inquisitor in Rome for having burned a number of books which included writings by Erasmus and a copy of the Decameron by *Boccaccio*.[37]

In 1591 Bishop Tommaso Gargallo banned all books on astrology, necromancy, palmistry and other forms of divination and condemned all those who exercised magical arts.[38] On their part individual Inquisitors issued edicts – like the one issued by Inquisitor del Bufalo on 26 June 1596 – in which they ordered anyone, who owned or perused books included in the Index, to report the matter within twenty days.[39] This enabled the Holy Office to gain total control of the lives of all inhabitants from knights of the Order, or landowners, to the lowliest slave. The inhabitants were even supposed to ask their confessor whether they should report sinners to the Inquisitor.[40] It brought the risk of false testimony, cast doubts upon the trustworthiness of witnesses, and easily allowed minor infringements to swell into heresy. Inevitably, a tendency such as this further strenghtened the far-reaching arm of the Inquisition in Malta.[41]

Thus the Magnifico Bartholomeo de Pomodoro of Valletta asked a corsair, who had just returned from Barbary, whether he had anything to sell. The corsair had only brought with him two or

---

36 Ibid., 4A, case 5, fols.33-36: 12 November, 1577.

37 AIM Corr, t.88, Tomo I: (1577-1636), fol.1.

38 P. Cassar, *Medical History of Malta*, p.426.

39 *...comandiamo et ordiniamo a tutti di qualsiasi voglia grado... et religione... che tra termino di 20 giorni ci debbano portare la lista di tutti libri prohibiti sotto pena oltre l'altri expressi nelli sacri canoni di Pontefici di scomunica recando tutte le licenze date da noi o da nostri predecessori di legere, o tenere tanto la sacra scrittura... volgare quanto altri libri di qualsivoglia materia... Datum Melitae In civitate Valletta et inedibus nostre solite residentia. Die xxvi mensis Junii 1596. Innocentius Bubalus.* AIM Proc Crim. Vol. 14B, case 45, fol.754.

40 *In un'isola attaccatissima alle tradizioni cristiane, le fantasie del popolo diventano molto suscetibili a qualche scandalo publico contro il buon costume.* A. Bonnici, *Aspetti della vita cristiana nell'isola di Malta verso la metà del seicento*, p.10.

41 C. Cassar, 'The Reformation and sixteenth century Malta', p.64.

three boxes with a large quantity of 'Moorish books' *gran quantità di libri moreschi* of which he had only sold one for 20 scudi.[42] The owner of this book was intercepted and the work was passed on to the engineer Fra Vittorio Cassar, who seems to have gained some knowledge of Arabic. Cassar asserted that the book *non tratta d'altro se non de geomancia, aeromancia, hydromancia e pyromancia, sensa le figure ma per via di versi.*[43]

Nonetheless, there continued to be a clientele for occult titles, and such works frequently surfaced in trials, whether for magical or other crimes.[44] The procedure of keeping a close watch on printed matter that entered the Harbour of Malta seems to have been further enforced at the turn of the century. Above all else, the Inquisition records reveal that the Tribunal perceived writing and literacy as a potential promoter both of heretical behaviour and social protest among the laity which the Church deemed as threats that had to be controlled. Even scribbling was a suspicious act and had to be reported to the Inquisitor.

In February 1600, the lawyer and officer of the Civil Law Courts Bartholomeo Habela, noted several doodles and verses from the Bible scribbled on the front page of the register of imported goods for the year 1598-1599. He considered these writings as 'very suspicious' and immediately denounced the matter to the Inquisition.[45] Several Law Courts employees were called to give witness, and admitted that they had the habit of scribbling doodles on the front page of each register in order to recognize the contents. It soon became known that the writings were the work of the Sicilian Antonino Cavaleri who was later sentenced to pay two *scudi* to the

---

[42] AIM Proc Crim. 17, case 132, fol.347: 17 August 1599.

[43] '...this book, which you show to me, deals with geomancy, aeromancy, hydromancy and pyromancy, in verse without the use of figures'. AIM Proc Crim. 17, case 132, fol.349: 19 August 1599.

[44] P.F. Grendler, *The Roman Inquisition and the Venetian Press*, p.196.

[45] AIM Proc Crim. 147B, item 20, fol.319: 18 February 1600.

Confraternity of the Rosary of the Annunciation Church in Vittoriosa.[46]

The Inquisition records reveal that the Tribunal perceived writing and literacy as potentially a promoter of both heretical belief and social protest among the laity. From the Church's point of view, the literate laity presented as many problems as the illiterates. Thanks to the spread of printing presses, literacy appears to have spread throughout Christendom – a trend confirmed by the number of individuals appearing before the Inquisition Tribunal – and accused of owning or perusing prohibited books throughout Catholic Europe.[47] In reality, by the middle of the sixteenth century, the printed book had been produced in sufficient quantities to become accessible to anyone who could read. The case of Antonino Cavaleri provides concrete evidence that by the end of that century the Catholic Church – through the workings of the Inquisition – had managed to control the lives, and most inner thoughts, of Malta's inhabitants.

---

46 Antonino Cavaleri was a Sicilian from Licata, aged 35, and married to a Maltese girl. He lived in Valletta and had been serving the Civil Law Courts, better known as Magna Curia Castel-lania for about five years. He admitted *solamente ci era depinta quella botte la quale si sol fare per un segno per conoscere la continentia del quinterno stante che ci son parechi sorti di quinterni*...Ibid., fols.322: 23 February, 1600. Sentence on fol. 327: 20 June 1600.

47 C. Ginzburg, *The Cheese and the Worms*, pp.29-30.

Ha Tanti Libri e sa
Quanto un Demonio

In what perhaps is the only scholarly study in Maltese historiography on the role of Vittorio Cassar – son of the Maltese military
engineer and architect Gerolamo Cassar – V. Mallia-Milanes
asserts that while Maltese researchers have managed to throw
light on Gerolamo,[1] we still have learnt very little about his elder
son, Vittorio.[2] Mallia-Milanes justifies his analysis 'in view of what
has hitherto appeared to be the relative rarity of surviving evidence

---

[1] See for example: R. de Giorgio, 'Advice on the Fortification of Mount Sceberras including
Gerolamo Cassar's contribution to their improvement', pp.73-95; E. Sammut, 'Girolamo Cassar,
Architect of Valletta', pp.22-34; G. Mangion, 'Girolamo Cassar, 'Architetto maltese del cinquecento', pp.192-200. Between 1981-1982, while employed as Research Assistant at the Cathedral
Archives, the present writer had the task of sorting out most of the Civil proceedings of the
Inquisition Tribunal and those of the *Reverenda Fabrica di S. Pietro*. Due to the disorder they
were in, these archives had previously been inaccessible to the general public. Among the manuscripts discovered by the author, there was a petition by Mattia Cassar, widow of Gerolamo dated
7 October 1597, which enables us to gain unique insights into the activities of the engineer and
provides the only reliable date for the death of Gerolamo Cassar: *detto de Cassar qual ha servito
per molti anni inanzi al assedio insino al Anno 1592 et in quel crudellissimo et inaudito assedio
di Turchi et altri barbari dove non spaccagnando presento la persona ha resarcito le rovine fatti
dalli inimici per sicurta delli nostri dalli quotidiani assalti terribili. Et dopo detto assedio si
ritrovo dalla prima linea nel edifitione di questa citta Valletta procurando co ogni affectione...
a perfectioni si importante fortezza... similmente ha disegnato tutti li edifitii che in essa si
trovano non ha mancato ancora di mettere in bona forma la citta Vittoriosa la fortezza della
Senglea similmente nella citta vecchia e nel Gozzo e finalmente per tutta l'isola dove fu di
bisogno con grandissimi suoi travagli ha resarcito e servito per il che lo Ill.mo Cardinale...
(Grand Master Verdalle 1582-1595), Gran Maestro li concesse sei salmate di terreno per ricom-
pensa di tanti suoi travagli...* AIM Proc Civ 7 case 15, fol.67: 7 October 1597.

[2] V. Mallia-Milanes, 'In search of Vittorio Cassar. A documentary approach', p.247.

on Vittorio Cassar'.[3] Within this context Mallia-Milanes reproduces a
series of 29 documents dating between 1586 and 1606, extracted from
several archives, in which he manages to portray Vittorio Cassar as a
worthy son of his gifted father.[4] Of particular interest are the documents relating to the character of Vittorio Cassar. Mallia-Milanes
appears to agree with the opinion of E. Schermerhorn that 'Fra
Vittorio was of a difficult temperament, ever on the alert for affronts
and provocations' that often led to embittered quarrels and criminal
offences.[5] We thus learn that the engineer was imprisoned twice by
the Order's government. On 12 November 1593 he was imprisoned for
two months *ad carcerem turris* for wounding his maternal uncle
Brandano Cassia.[6] On 5 December 1594 he was again imprisoned for
six months at Fort St Angelo, 'for having used stones to hammer upon
the bedroom windows of Fra Emmanuele de Carnero's residence and
beaten his domestic servant'.[7] Mallia-Milanes also reveals another
interesting aspect of Vittorio Cassar's character:

> On at least two occasions, one in 1602, which refers back to the 1590s, the
> other in 1606, he was accused at the Court of the Inquisition of having been
> involved in fortune telling. On both occasions… he was sought after for his
> reputed powers of relieving people of their state of anxiety, of reassuring
> them and of reading their future.[8]

Further in-depth analyses of the Inquisition archives has revealed
more valuable information on Vittorio Cassar's qualities, not just as
the principal architect and engineer living in Malta after his father's
demise, but also as necromancer, diviner, healer and exorcist.

A Necromancer and Man of Learning

Fra Vittorio seems to have been influenced by Francesco Giorgi's
work *De Harmonia Mundi* first published in 1525. Giorgi, as a
Christian Cabalist, believed that the *Cabala* could prove the truth

---

[3] Ibid.

[4] Ibid., pp.261-69.

[5] Ibid., p.249; E. Schermerhorn, *Malta of the Knights*, p.81.

[6] V. Mallia-Milanes, 'In search of Vittorio Cassar', p.249; cf. NLM AOM 98, fol.130v.

[7] Ibid.; NLM AOM 98, fol.190.

[8] V. Mallia-Milanes, 'In Search of Vittorio Cassar', p.250.

of Christianity. The connection would be better understood if one keeps in mind the Neoplatonist theories of the time in which the Vitruvian architecture figured prominently. For Giorgi it had a religious significance connected with the Temple of Solomon.[9]

In 1601 Vittorio Cassar admitted to the Inquisition that he kept and perused several prohibited books which he said were received from a friend of his in Messina called Mastro Gioanne Mancuso – a brass-worker. Three of the books, namely, *La Clavicola di Solomone*; *De Mansionibus Lune* by Pietro Baiolardi and another book by Pietro Debano (presumably D'Abano) were in manuscript form. According to Cassar, Mancuso was looking for someone who could make use of the experiments they contained. Vittorio said that, at the time, he had been sent to Gozo *per far fare la fortalezza* and since Don Antonio Attardo would not absolve him during confession, he handed the books to the Inquisition for burning.[10]

In a spontaneous comparition before the Inquisition Tribunal on 5 June 1605, Fra Vittorio explained among other things that when his father, Gerolamo, was still alive, he had made use of a recipe found in one of his father's books that could be applied on women in difficult labour. The remedy consisted in giving a crust of bread to the sick woman on which the words: + *Jesus* + *Natus* + were written accompanied by the recitation of three *Ave Maria*s and three *Pater Noster*s. Fra Vittorio admitted to have adoperated the remedy twice. Once to the daughter of Fra Simon Provost, the Master of the Mint, and on another occasion to one of his neighbours in Valletta.[11]

Apparently Cassar remained obsessed with books on necromancy and other related subjects till his death. On 24 April 1609, Pietro

[9] D.P. Walker, *Spiritual and Demonic Magic*, pp.112-119.

[10] AIM Proc Crim 26A, case 182, fol.273v.

[11] Ibid., fol.273. Provost, another professed member of the Order, 'kept a concubine, Isabella, since the siege of 1565... From this relationship he had a daughter, Lucretia, but although he sustained both mother and daughter, he did not keep them at home'. For more information consult: C. Cassar, 'The Reformation and sixteenth century Malta', pp.51-68.

De Armenia of Valletta[12] referred to a discussion he had had with a prostitute named Gioanna La Siracusana, who claimed to be the carnal friend of Fra Vittorio Cassar. Gioanna declared that the year before, she had intentionally absented herself from Malta, out of fear of the Inquisition, since she learned that Fra Vittorio had a collection of writings and books on magic. But although she did declare that he kept such books and writings at home, she could not say what they contained.[13] Evidently Cassar's girl friend was illiterate.

As has already been stated, the possession of, and trade in such books were prohibited by the Church. Yet there seems to have been a relatively substantial demand for occult titles. The popularity of *La Clavicola di Solomone* has already been pointed out. We also learn that Tiberio Camarda had at some point attempted to steal *La Clavicola di Solomone* from Cassar *perche haverebbe cavato gran frutto di quella.*[14] However, it is interesting to note that Cassar was aware of the work by the medieval magician Pietro d'Abano 'whose operations were directed to the angels or spirits of planets, with the purpose of compelling them to do something extraordinary'.[15] At the same time, Pietro Baiolardo was considered to be a magician

---

[12] Pietro De Armenia was the son of Mario De Armenia, the Vice-Portulano of the *Università* (Town Council of Mdina) and the grandson of Luca De Armenia author of the Latin poem written on the eve of the Siege of 1565. C. Cassar, "*'O Melita Infelix'*" – A poem on the great siege written in 1565'; D. Cutajar & C. Cassar, 'Malta and the sixteenth century struggle for the Mediterranean', pp.38-40.

[13] AIM Proc Crim. 33B case 444, fol.698. On 22 January 1609, Mariano Deadriano reported that Vittorio Cassar had explained the whole matter in some detail. Cassar had in fact planned Gioanna's trip to Naples in order that she would not be interrogated by the Holy Office. Ibid., 28B, case 197, fols.843; See: Appendix IIIA.

[14] Ibid., vol 15B, case 111 fol.659v: 10 October 1596. Camarda seems to have attributed strong powers to reading. On one occasion he related that at Messina he went for a walk in a garden in the company of several young men among whom was the cousin of the Count of Cabuso. The latter asked those present whether they were interested to go to Venice. As soon as one of them agreed, the cousin of the Count drew a circle on the ground and started to read from a book. There soon appeared a number of devils disguised as dogs and several dark clouds which obscured the place. One of those present was so frightened that he died soon afterwards. Ibid., fol.660v.

[15] D.P. Walker, *Spiritual and Demonic Magic*, p.86.

of such great powers that in nineteenth century Sicily, the eminent ethnographer G. Pitré, could still recall the phrase: *cumannari li Diavuli comu Pietru Bailardu* (Commanding the Devils like Pietro Baiolardo).[16] In other words, the three texts must have made great impact on Cassar's activities as a magician. No wonder Cassar was often accused of practising necromancy.

There are indications that Vittorio Cassar was considered as a gentleman of great learning. In January 1597 Vincentio Xerri recalled a discussion which he had with Bernardo La Vechia and the deceased Augustino Cassar on board the Capitana galley while at anchorage in Messina. One of his mates declared *che fra Vittorio Cassar figlio del quondam Geronimo lo Ingegneri sapeva fare delle magarie.*[17] Augustino had asserted that on consulting Fra Vittorio for love magic, Fra Vittorio gave him a bone which he had to burn in front of his lady love. Augustino even stated that Fra Vittorio had a box which was full of *imbarazzi di magarie* (things related to magic), adding that Fra Vittorio had the habit of cutting pieces of flesh from the corpses of those that had been hanged, drawn and quartered.[18] The following year the Catalan knight Fra Bartolomeo Brul confirmed that Fra Vittorio had in time become a popular topic of gossip. In a conversation that Fra Brul had had with several Castilian knights, it was rumored that Fra Vittorio had attempted an experiment which would liberate him and the other inmates from imprisonment at St Elmo.[19]

Rumours about Fra Vittorio's abilities spread far and wide in Malta. Salvo Camilleri recomended to Martino Burlo of Vittoriosa to resort to Fra Vittorio for love magic because 'Fra Vittorio Cassar

[16] G. Pitré, *Usi e Costumi, Credenze e Pregiuzizi del Popolo Siciliano.* IV, p.96; G. Cocchiara, *Il Diavolo nella Tradizione Popolare Italiana*, p.189, n.99.

[17] 'that Fra Vittorio Cassar, son of the deceased engineer Geronimo, knew how to adoperate magic'. AIM Proc Crim. 15A, case 97, fol.511.

[18] Ibid., fol.511v.

[19] *...me parse che don Alonso Bricegno habbi detto allora come detto Vittorio stando carcerato in Santo Helmo con certi preti li disse una sera, volete che ni andamo da questi carceri et dicendoli essi si, li disse adunque starrete quieti et non vi movete quando sentite alcun rumore, et lui mettendo certa polvere legeva, et mettendo fuoco nella polvere quelli si mossero, et lui li disse, non havemo adunque fatto niente doppo voi vi sete movuti.* AIM Proc Crim. 16A, case 10, fol.144: 17 August 1598.)

knows very well what remedies should be given to similar persons'. Besides 'Fra Vittorio even keeps a demon in a jug which he has locked in his room'.[20]

His repute as necromancer was so great, that once a school-boy found it convenient to attribute an experiment he had invented to Fra Vittorio. In July 1606, Francesco de Gaeta – a sixteen-year-old boy who was then attending the school of Giacomo Xerri in the vicinity of the Jesuit Church in Valletta – declared that one of his school-mates, Gio. Luigi Metaxi, had practised divination by designing the shape of the earth. Metaxi drew several geometrical lines writing down the names of several planets to figure out when de Gaeta would leave Malta. Metaxi declared to his friend that he had learned the experiment from Fra Vittorio.[21] When summoned in front of the Inquisitor, Metaxi asserted that since he heard that Fra Vittorio makes divination, he had told de Gaeta *gli dissi anco che detto secreto m'havevo imparato il detto Fra Vittorio Cassar si bene non e vero nemmeno il detto secreto, ma lo fu inventione mia per burlarli.*[22]

In reality, Cassar had an inquisitive mind and he did not miss an opportunity to discuss and learn new concepts in science, engineering or otherwise. Such an impression is best gained from a case dated December 1604 when Cassar, accompanied by his brother Fra Gabriele, was reported to have visited the Orders' ovens in Valletta with the intention of examining the newly installed mill. At the oven, the two Cassar brothers seem to have had a stimulating discussion with Cosimo Lo Furno, the Sicilian gentleman, inventor of the new machine.[23] Cosimo told Fra Vittorio that he knew a lot of secrets and prided himself in being well informed of what was going on in Rome, adding that he even knew a secret on how to

---

[20] AIM Proc Crim. 20B, case 98, fol.393: 2 April, 1602.

[21] AIM Proc Crim. 28B, case 193, fol.608.

[22] 'I also told him that I had learned the secret from Fra Vittorio Cassar even though the secret is not true but I invented it to fool them' (his school mates). Ibid., fols.609v-10: 19 July 1606.

[23] Ibid., Vol.23B case 366, fol.639.

repel an invasion.[24] When called to give witness before the Holy
Office, Fra Vittorio admitted that Cosimo and himself had
discussed *artificii di foco* (firing equipment) and other machines
and architecture.[25] It thus transpires that Fra Vittorio considered
himself to be, above all else, a man of science of which magic then
formed an integral part.

Vittorio Cassar and Islam

But Cassar's formation as necromancer is unique, since it was not
only based on the learned magic of the Renaissance, but he
managed to combine his Christian beliefs with the beliefs and practices of the Muslim world. Cassar obviously had access to this
culture due to the presence of a multitude of Muslim slaves that
were annually captured in the crusading activities of the Order of
St John. 'By 1590 slaves (in Malta) numbered around 3,000'.[26]

Thanks to the presence of the Muslim slaves, it was possible for
Vittorio Cassar to learn Arabic and he was often called upon and
requested by the Inquisition to describe the contents of Arabic
books that were confiscated and perused on the island. In a case
against the 'Moor' called Hambar, slave of the Bailiff Fra Federico
Cozza, Cassar admits

> *per la pratticha che io ho della lingua (araba), et anco simil sorte de*
> *fatture che sogliono fare i mori per essermene passate molte altre (scritte)*
> *per le mani si come vostra Signoria che mi ha fatto chiamare altre volte*
> *per il detto effetto.*[27]

---

[24] Ibid., fol.639v; Rome was considered to be the centre of all creative activities in Catholic
southern Europe. Indeed Fernand Braudel, in his masterpiece on the Mediterranean, asserts
that 'Rome was a great centre of cultural diffusion, by no means the only one, but certainly the
most important'. F. Braudel, *The Mediterranean and the Mediterranean World in the Age of
Philip II*. Vol.II, p.829.

[25] Ibid., fol.640v: 22 December 1604.

[26] C. Cassar, 'Popular perceptions and values in Hospitaller Malta', p.434. See also: G.
Wettinger, 'Some aspects of slavery in Malta, 1530-1800'.

[27] 'thanks to my knowledge of Arabic, as well as the magic which is usually practiced by Moors,
which your Lordship knows very well since you have called me on other occasions for this
effect'. AIM Proc Crim. 17, case 110, fol. 260: 5 November 1600.)

Cassar seems to have been considered as the Arabic language 'expert' of the Tribunal.[28] In a letter from Gozo dated 22 July 1601, he asserts that he was unable to leave the sister island in order to examine some Arabic texts, since the Council of the Order instructed him to return to Gozo without delay. At the time he seems to have spent most of his time in Gozo, at least the middle months of the year 1600.[29] In Gozo, Cassar appears to have participated fully in the activities that took place there.[30]

Cassar admitted to have learned how to read and write Arabic from a Moor by the name of Sellem, a slave of the Order of St John, who walked with the aid of crutches due to a fall in which he broke both his legs. Sellem had been teaching Cassar for several years and had even offered to teach him divination by invocating the

---

[28] This did not exempt him from being imprisoned at the instigation of the Inquisitor. Besides, Cassar did not seem to nurture any special respect for the Tribunal and likewise for the Inquisitor. When on 15 August 1596 he was released from St Elmo for the feast of the Annunciation, Cassar was reported to have said publicly – *dove ci erano quasi la maggior parte delli soldati di detta fortezza* – (where there was present the great majority of the soldiers of that fortress) that in order to be released he had to pay eighty *scudi* which was meant to be used for pious works. (AIM Proc Crim. 15A, case 77, fol.337: 8 October, 1596). On 8 November he declared in front of the Inquisitor: *Io sonno uxito perche quelli signori volevano che Io facesse alcuni disegni e mi vennero a chiamare molti volti e poi in lingua fui posto di caroana e perche ci era ordine che tutti quelli che eran posti in caroana andassero percio Io uxi fuori per andare di caroana.* (I was released because I was asked to prepare some plans and I have been called many a time besides the fact that the Langue [i.e. the Langue of Castile to which he belonged] had insisted with me many a time to go on the caruane and so I left [the prison] to go on a caruana (Ibid., fol.338v.). Later in his trial he admitted to have said so *per mia sciochezza* (due to my foolishness) (Ibid., fol.339v). Vittorio Cassar was made to fast every Friday for a year and confess at the beginning of Lent, on Whitsunday, on Annunciation day and on Christmas day. On the suggestion of his confessor he had to receive Holy Communion on such feasts. During the year of penance he had to present himself twice a week in front of the Inquisitor. (Ibid., fols.342-v: 11 February, 1597)

[29] Ibid., 20B, case 130, fol.708. On 31 January 1602 he asserts: *Da un anno e mezzo inqua io retrovandome a fare la fortalezza di questo Castello del Gozzo come architetto* (For the last one and a half years I have worked on the fortifications of the Gozo Castle as an architect). Ibid., fol.709.

[30] Vittorio Cassar was present when the son of Mariano Metallo offended Reverend Antonio Dallo by saying that he will ask the Pope to stop him from saying mass and burn him at the stake. Ibid., 23A case 300: 13 July 1602.

stars in order to learn the future. Cassar admitted to have tried
experiments on divination and even presented a copy book which
was used for studying the lessons. He added that he considered
divination as useless, even though he had practised it several
times. But that was before he learned that such practices were
prohibited by the Church. Finally Cassar stated that Sellem had
tried to teach him necromancy which he said in Arabic is called
reuchamia, but he did not want to know anything about it since he
knew that it was prohibited.[31] Obviously Cassar must have relied
on the general belief *che detti mori facessero detti remedii operare
per via di magarie, per virtù del demonio... Io intendo dire publica-
mente in piazza che questo moro xich Selem sia publico magaro et
maleficio...* as was earlier related by Mastro Dionisio Cardona.[32]

On his part, Sellem ben Mansur – an Egyptian from Cairo who at
the time of his deposition declared himself to be about forty years
of age – admitted that he knew how to read and write in Arabic and
that he practised astrology which he refers to as *chot ir-ramel*. He
asserted that he came from a family of astrologers and that he had
learned the 'profession' from his father. He added that Fra Vittorio
Cassar had visited him thirty or forty days before, and asked
Sellem to teach him astrology. Sellem obliged and gave Cassar
several lessons, but was not sure whether Cassar had understood
what he tried to teach him.[33]

The Obsessive Search for Hidden Treasure

The search for hidden treasure may be considered as a major obsession of the sixteenth century élite. It whetted the apetite of lawyers,
notaries, priests and friars who practised demonic magic. Local

---

[31] Ibid., 26A case 182, fol.272-v: 5 June 1605.

[32] 'that these Moors make the said remedies operate by means of magic, by virtue of the devil...
I hear people say in the public square that this Moor Xich Selem is a public wizard'.
Deposition given by Mastro Dionisio Cardona, a carpenter from Senglea. Ibid., fol.303.

[33] Ibid., fols.295-v: 28 June 1605.

fables frequently indicated ruined houses, or chapels as sites of buried treasure. Actual licences for the search of treasure trove were issued by several sixteenth century Grand Masters. In 1530 one such licence was issued to Luca De Armenia and Antonio Callus to search for gold and silver hoards;[34] in 1537 a similar licence was issued to the medical doctor Giuseppe Callus;[35] in 1536 (?) permission was given to Petro Calava;[36] and finally Fra Simon Provost, Master of the Mint, was given permission to look for hidden treasure together with Gaspare Mombron, Antonuccio Bonello and others, on condition that one-third of their finds were to be handed to the Order's treasury.[37] After all, hoards had already been discovered before the advent of the Hospitaller Order in 1530. G. Wettinger points out that in 1525 a trove consisting of about thirteen pounds weight of Byzantine gold coins was discovered.[38]

The Franciscan Friar Minor, Fra Pietro di Malta, was obsessed with the idea of buried treasures. He was made to believe, by two of his friends, that in the chapel of St Paul the Hermit (sited at Wied il-Għasel, Mosta) there was a hidden treasure.[39] Such beliefs were not unfounded since excess cash was often deposited underground for safekeeping and such hoards occasionally turned up accidentally.[40]

---

[34] NLM AOM 414, fol.285v:14 December, 1530. cf. G. Wettinger, *The Jews of Malta*, p.152 n.56 for evidence on licences for the search of hidden treasure in 1530, 1537 and 1582. 'Malta has been an archaelogical hunting ground for many centuries. People have always sought hidden treasure and sometimes it has been discovered by accident, as in the case of the little *pichulilli* who found a hoard of 248 Byzantine gold pieces in 1458/9... in 1530 Luca De Armenia and Antonio Callus even received a licence to seek ancient treasure of gold and silver'. A.T. Luttrell, 'Approaches to Medieval Malta', p.11.

[35] NLM AOM 416, fol.220v: 27 August, 1537.

[36] Ibid., 13 October, 1536 (?)

[37] NLM AOM 440, fol.252: 20 March, 1582.

[38] G. Wettinger, 'The Gold hoard of 1525', pp.25-33.

[39] AIM Proc Crim., 20A, case 70, fols.24-26.

[40] On 12 April 1698, whilst digging in the pavement of a house at Mdina, which had to be pulled down in order to make room for the present Cathedral square, a worker discovered a copper jar full of gold coins weighing eighteen pounds. G.A. Ciantar, *Malta Illustrata*, Vol.II. pp.96-7. See also G. Wettinger, *The Jews of Malta*, p.147.

There was not necessarily anything magical about the search for hidden treasure, but the assistance of a conjuror – often a Muslim slave who practised divination – was frequently invoked. The combination of gullibility and greed sometimes led people to foolish lengths, and people from all quarters of society used magical techniques to separate people from their money. The Canon of the Mdina Cathedral, Don Ambrosio Pace, had heard several rumours from *parecchi vecchi e homini antiani* (several old men) that his house had originally belonged to Jews and that it should therefore contain a buried treasure since in the past several Jews had lived at Mdina. One day while at home he started to search for the treasure by digging in a corner of a room at the basement without any success. Sometime later, a Cypriot Greek suggested to Don Ambrosio that he should consult with a Muslim galley-slave who was an expert in such matters. The slave was brought over and he began to pace all over the basement while reading from a book. Owning and perusing the right book, however, was only the beginning of the search. The magician had then to locate the potential site of treasure. He therefore asked Don Ambrosio to provide him with a plate in which he deposited a piece of gold and one of silver given to him by the owner of that house and insisted that the treasure was hidden in the area where Don Ambrosio had dug. For this service, the galley-slave obtained a gold ring and added that he needed the help of another slave. When the slave-magician returned accompanied by his friend, he asked for a black hen – which had to be killed in the trench – and another ring, both of which were provided by Don Ambrosio. At this point however, the Canon realised that he was being fooled and turned them out of his house.[41] Gaspare Bonnichi from Vittoriosa had similarly been fooled by a galley-slave who used the same kind of divination.[42]

Yet people did not always resort to Muslim slaves to look for hidden treasure. In 1596 the painter Mattheo Stagno of Valletta confessed that he had been invited by the French knight Fra Aboglion to help Fra Vittorio Cassar search for treasure in a plot of land which Cassar owned in Birkirkara. He stated that those

---

[41] AIM Proc Crim. 22C, case 234 fols.938-39v: 17 March 1604.
[42] Ibid., 19A, case 28, fol.203-204: 8 April 1601.

present included Jacobo Caminici from Vittoriosa and Jachi Francese (cook of the Prior of Naples). On their arrival on the site, Fra Vittorio placed four swords in the form of a cross and kneeling down, he started reading slowly from a book. His companions put blessed palm branches on the cross.[43]

A few days later, the French knight Fra Gabriel Lepetit asserted that from the moment he had obtained permission from the Grand Master to seek buried treasure, many Maltese revealed to him that in an area of Birkirkara, there was a treasure buried and that Cassar was the first to approach him. On his part, Fra Vittorio recalled how his father Gerolamo knew about the existence of this treasure and had once told him that in the Church of Santa Sophia in Constantinople they keep record of all treasures and for that reason he had bought that particular area of land.[44] In order to identify the spot, Gerolamo put four large stones, but since his death, during the reign of Grand Master Verdalle (1582-1595), Fra Vittorio had not bothered to look for treasure. Not long afterwards Fra Lepetit, accompanied by Cassar, spent many a night looking for treasure in that area. The French knight admitted that this went on for three continuous months and that the area had originally belonged to 'the governor of the Jews'. In the course of the search, both Fra Vittorio and himself had heard a lot of noise and had seen a black man and a horse in that place. But although they had dug up parts of that area, they had failed to find any hidden treasure.[45]

Sorcerer, Healer and Diviner

On 19 October 1596, Mario Xuereb reported a discussion, for which he was present, between Tiberio Camarda and his friend Julio

---

[43] Ibid., 14B case 38, fols.673-v: 7 June 1596.

[44] Vittorio Cassar later explained that his father had received a letter from Constantinople from a learned Moor which said that in the area known as Santa Domenica there was a buried treasure which had been hidden by the Jews. Ibid., fols.688v-89: 18 June 1596.

[45] Ibid., fols.681-81: 15 June 1596. Inquisitor Bufalo condemned Fra Vittorio to six months imprisonment at Fort St Elmo, during which time had had to confess and receive Holy Communion on the feasts of the Assumption, and on All Saints Day. He also had to recite the rosary every Saturday. Ibid., fols.691-91v: 10 July 1596.

Cassia. The three of them were imprisoned in the same cell at the Grand Master's prisons, where Camarda admitted that he had learned a great deal on necromancy from Fra Vittorio. Amongst other details, he had learned how to 'accommodate' a bone taken from the body of a hanged man on which he wrote an invocation starting with the words *scongiuro vos*.[46] Cassar was reputed to have taught Camarda how to invoke the spirits in order to search for buried treasure and how to employ ink on the finger nails of a pregnant woman or a virgin which had to be accompanied by prayers (including three *Paster Noster*s and *Ave Maria*s) and then invoke an evil spirit from whom he could learn anything he wanted to know, to alleviate his miseries, to attract women and even to endure torture. Tiberio even kept on his own person a paper in an unknown script which would help him overcome his rival in a duel.[47]

Cassar's reputation as sorcerer seems to have remained strong in later years among those who had to endure torture. In March 1607, a young Maltese man named Alessandro alias *Elefante* – imprisoned at the Grand Master's prisons and awaiting to be tortured by means of the *corda*[48] – asked Vittorio Cassar to prepare a potion that could make him bear the pains of torture so that he would not be forced to confess.[49]

It appears that Fra Vittorio took pride in his role as necromancer. Mariano Deadriano, a Sicilian from Castrogiovanni (modern Enna), who served as clerk in the building of the Gozo fort (Forte Garzes

---

[46] Ibid., 15B, case 111 fols.659, 669.

[47] Ibid., fol.669-69v: 19 October 1596.

[48] 'The most generally used kind of torture was the *strappado*, *corda* or *cola*, called by jurists the "queen of torments". The accused's hands were tied behind the back, attached to a rope which was thrown over a beam in the ceiling, and hauled into the air, there to hang for a period of time, then let down, then raised again. Sometimes weights were attached to the feet of the accused, therefore increasing the strain on the arm and back muscles once the process was begun'. E. Peters, Torture, Oxford, 1985. p.68.

[49] AIM Proc Crim. 28B, case 197 fol.836: 26 March 1607. On 15 April, Gio. Petro Mamo stated that five months before, while passing by the house of Vittorio Cassar in Valletta accompanied by the cleric Claudio Catone, he noticed that Fra Vittorio was talking to a woman whom Catone recognized as the mother of Alessandro *elefante* who was in prison. Mamo added that Alessandro's mother must have surely been asking Fra Vittorio some remedy to alleviate her son's miseries since his brother-in-law, Mastro Antonio Mawodi, had resorted to Fra Vittorio's remedies when faced with *strappado*. Ibid., fol.841.

at Mġarr harbour [Gozo]), considered himself a good friend and close associate of Fra Vittorio the architect of that project. Fra Vittorio often had long discussions with the Sicilian clerk and confided many secrets to him. Amongst others Fra Vittorio admitted that he knew enough secrets on necromancy and magic that he could get in touch with the devils and spirits whenever he wished. He added that he had a good number of books on necromancy and magic which he hid in order not to be confiscated by the Inquisition. Cassar even agreed to teach necromancy to two of his friends from Messina and who had spent some time with him in Gozo. Deadriano further added that Vittorio Cassar was *gran magaro* (a great wizard). Mariano also stated that Vittorio could communicate with the spirits by putting some ink on the palm of the hand of a virgin boy, and by proferring several words, he could command the spirits to comply with his wishes and to make him win in games.[50]

The evidence given by Deadriano seems to contain a strong element of truth. A couple of years earlier, the French knight Fra Antonio Ghijon declared that *per le tante preghiere* (due to the many pleadings), Fra Vittorio agreed to adoperate divination in order to win in the game of dice. Fra Ghijon added that he had resorted to divination techniques because he had lost a sum of nine hundred scudi to another French knight Fra Musu La Lea. Fra Ghijon further believed that *detto cavaliere guadagnava al gioco con qualche artificio e virtu diabolica per il che io mi pigliai gran dolore*.[51] Thus a few days later, in the vicinity of the Carmelite Church in Valletta, he met Cassar in the house of a Greek woman called Lucretia. On this occasion Fra Vittorio adoperated palmistry on a nine year old girl by writing with ink on her hands and after having smeared her thumbs with oil, interrogated her on Fra Ghijon's losing such a hefty sum of money in dice games. The girl declared that she could see

---

[50] Ibid., fols.843-44: 22 January 1609; Appendix IIIA.

[51] 'the said knight gained in games by some mechanisms and diabolical virtues for which I am very sorry'. Ibid., 169, case 87, fol.4: 14 April 1607.

*un personaggio ben vestito con una corona al capo, e molte altre persone
che lo seguitavano... ma noi non potevamo vedere cosa alcuna e detto Fra
Vittorio disse che la causa era perche io e lui non eramo vergini, ma la
figliola le vedeva perche era vergine... e la figliola disse che quelli spiriti
gli respondeano e in particolare quello della corona gli diceva, che detto
cavaliere mi havea guadagnato detti danari al gioco con arte diabolica
stante che teneva un spirito astretto in un anello che portava al deto
piccolo della man destra...*[52]

The belief in spirits, present in daily life, formed the basis on which
both popular and learned magic could develop, for it was possible to
use their supernatural powers to protect oneself from aggression,
predict the future or acquire wealth or love.[53] Obviously the Church
considered consultation with the spirits as the type of divination
technique that was potentially the most dangerous. Fortune-telling
was particularly sinister, since it was often connected with sorcery
and the casting of spells. Witch beliefs were particularly widespread since medical knowledge then proved inadequate, while
magic could always be put forward as an explanation.[54] In such
circumstances, Cassar seems to have adoperated a basic stereo-
typed method both for divination and healing purposes.

Probably Cassar's medical knowledge must have been influenced
by readings from the Greek writer Galen, who following Aristotle,
believed that man derives life from the vital spirits which travel from
the left ventricle of the heart to all parts of the body, including the
brain. One must keep in mind that the Church strongly prohibited
doctors to open up the human body. Since healing methods at the
time were mostly based on suppositions, it was normal for most
healers to believe that they could attain supernatural powers which
involved mystery. Thus Henciona, wife of Vittorio Cassar's cousin

---

[52] 'a well dressed character with a crown on his head and many other persons who made up his
retinue... but we could not see anything and Fra Vittorio said that the reason for this was that
we were not virgins, while the girl could see because she was a virgin... and the girl said that
the spirits were answering her questions and especially the crowned one who said that the
knight had managed to gain so much money in games by making use of diabolical arts as he
kept a spirit in a ring which he carried in the small finger of his right hand'. Ibid., fol.4v.

[53] J.M. Sallman, *Chercheurs de Trésors et Jeteuses de Sorts*, p.190 cf. D. Gentilcore, *From
Bishop to Witch*, p.226.

[54] C. Cassar, 'Witchcraft beliefs and social control', p.319.

Leonardo Gadineo, resorted to the expert necromancer to heal her fifteen-month-old daughter, after she had consulted several physicians without effect and had also requested to various priests and friars for exorcism, but no one could cure her daughter. Having visited the girl, Cassar asked his cousin-in-law to procure him a virgin girl, upon which Henciona admits:

> Io desiderosa della sanita di mia figlia, chiamai li in casa una figliola de Mastro Francesco Doneo chiamata Caterina d'anni otto mia vicina e detto Fra Vittorio gli prese il detto pollice della mano e gli raschio un poco l'ungio di quello, e con un poco d'olio comune che mi dimando gli l'onse, et interrogò detta figliola si vedeva qualche cosa nel ungio, e lei respose che vedeva una faccia allora detto Fra Vittorio gli disse e dimando in questa maniera che infirmita tiene questa figliola intendendo per la mia figlia, sara collera datagli nel latte della madre o mal de luna, e detta Caterina gli respondeva di no, allora dimando sara questa infirmita causata dalla parte di dietro ò davanti, del capo, e respose la figliola che l'infirmita veniva dalla parte de inanti del cerbro...[55]

According to the Provencal member of the Order, Fra Gioanni Forneri, Fra Vittorio applied palmistry even for love magic. Elaborating, Forneri said that Cassar called a young six-year-old boy who was passing by. He made him open the palm of his hand and started scribbling in ink and proferring several words from a book. But the experiment was not completed as the boy took fright and ran away.[56] But Cassar adopted the same type of divination techniques against the baneful influences of the evil eye which were

---

[55] 'Since I wished my daughter to return healthy, I invited at my home the daughter of Mastro Francesco Doneo my neighbour – an eight year old girl called Caterina. Fra Vittorio held her thumb in his hand and scraped the finger nail, then he put some ordinary oil and interrogated her on whether she could see anything on the finger nail. Caterina said that she could see a face at which Fra Vittorio asked her to ask what type of sickness the girl was suffering from, meaning my daughter, is it anger given to her in her mother's milk or else epilepsy, and the said Caterina answered no. Then he asked whether the disease is caused from the front or from the back, of the head and the girl answered that it came from front part of the brain'. AIM Proc Crim. 28B, case 197, fols.842-42v: 7 July 1608; Ibid., 28C, fols.1137-v: 5 July 1608.

[56] Ibid., 28B, case 197, fols.839-40: 6 April 1607.

threatening the relationship between two married partners. Margarita Liftech, who lived at the castello del Gozzo (Gozo Citadel), wanted to check whether her son-in-law, Bricio Cilia, had been induced to turn his attention to the love of a courtesan because he was *maleficiato*. On this occasion, Fra Vittorio made use of the services of a twelve-year-old girl who on having her nail thumbs smeared with oil asserted that she could see the shadows of two negro slaves.[57] Such activity suggests that the insecurity of married life was particularly felt by the wife who often remained at home under the tutelage of her mother, while the husband plied his trade away from the home.

A good example of this is provided by the mother and sister of Fra Vittorio himself. On 23 September 1596 Mathia, widow of *Mastro Gerolamo l'Ingegneri* and mother of Fra Vittorio, admitted to have adoperated a magical formula in aid of her sixteen year old daughter Marietta. Both women admitted that the previous year Marietta had been mistreated by her husband Natale Rizza who wanted to establish himself in Sicily. For this reason, the two women asked the help of a Moorish slave who prescribed the mixing of a consecrated host with her husband's wine.[58]

Vittorio Cassar and Popular Magic

Vittorio Cassar certainly looked down on popular magic. On 17 August 1596, he accused a Greek middle-aged woman named Calli to have practised magic by thrusting a black handled knife in an onion while proferring some secret. Cassar explained that Calli's intention was to hinder the galleys of the Order from departing from Malta since her carnal friend was sailing on one of them. He

---

[57] Ibid., case 196 fols. 829-30v: 11 September 1608. Another reference to this experiment on love magic: Ibid., 33A, case285, fols.82-3.

[58] The consecrated host was procured by Mathia with the aid of a Sicilian Dominican friar. The slave, demanded four *tari* for the advice, but Marietta gave him a gold ring which belonged to Mathia. The two women were imprisoned for their misdeed and were only released a month later, on 30 October. Ibid., 14B, case 54, fols.820-24. At that time Fra Vittorio was still imprisoned at Fort St Elmo Ibid., case 38, fols.672-93.

added *et in effetto il tempo fu cattivo e non si partero, e detta Calli
è una magara di importanza, che fa molte magarie.*[59] Cassar also
accused a close friend of Calli, Sevasti Landolina, who at one time
was the carnal friend of the Italian knight Bonviso. Sevastulla had
at one time asked Calli to prepare a love potion for her. Cassar even
accused the two women to have sprinkled salt in fire and thrust a
black handled knife in a flower pot while invoking the stars.[60] But
the worst accusation was directed against Sevastulla who reputedly kept a *manu pagana* – the hand of a pagan (probably meaning
non-Christian) infant wrapped in pearls, silk, coral, gold thread
and amber – in order to be loved by several men. Cassar asserted
that he had seen the *manu pagana* and believed that Calli had
procured it for Sevasti.[61]

That same month Vittorio Cassar was imprisoned at Fort St
Elmo by the Holy Office, presumably due to his activities as –
necromancer. He told several members of the St Elmo garrison that
the two women, Calli and Sevasti, had landed him in prison and
that he will have justice on his release.[62]

The relationship between popular and learned magic is a thorny
question which can yield a great deal of information on popular and
élite interactions in early modern Malta. It appears that in the
early years of the Order's rule, the illiterate and the literate worlds
were much closer, simply because belief in spirits and the supernatural formed the basis on which both learned and popular magic
could develop; 'for it was possible to use their supernatural powers

---

[59] 'and in effect the weather was bad and (the galleys) did not leave, and the said Calli is an
important witch who practices many magical experiments'. Ibid., 14B, case 60, fol. 858v: 17
August 1596.

[60] Ibid., fol.859.

[61] Cassar calls Calli, *publica magara, ruffiana e cortigiana* (public witch, pimp and courtesan).
Ibid., fols.859v-60.

[62] Indeed on 22 October 1596 Cali Corogna was scourged in several public squares in Valletta and
other towns, made to confess and receive Holy Communion four times a year for two years and
perpetually exiled from the Maltese islands. Sevasti Landolina was lightly tortured, made to
confess and receive Holy Communion for four years and was exiled from Valletta for eighteen
years. Ibid., fols.931-35v.

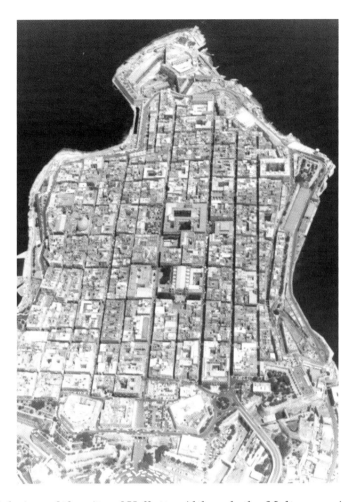

Aerial view of the city of Valletta. Although the Maltese engineer, Gerolamo Cassar, played the role of assistant to the Papal engineer Francesco Laparelli, Cassar was entrusted with the supervision of works on the Valletta fortifications and other major public edifices.

Photo – Department of Information.

Plate XVII

Portrait of Grand Master Hughes Loubenx de Verdalle (1582-1595). Grand Master Verdalle conceded six salme of land to the military engineer, Gerolamo Cassar, for the invaluable services rendered to the Order of St John in the building of the fortifications of Valletta.

Photo – Museum of Fine Arts, Valletta.

Plate XVIII

Aerial view of Fort St Angelo. Vittorio Cassar, eldest son of Gerolamo, was imprisoned twice by the Order's government. On one occassion he was kept for six months at Fort St Angelo.

Photo – Department of Information.

Plate XIX

Aerial view of Fort St Elmo. By 1598, Vittorio Cassar's abilities as a wizard were a popular subject of gossip. Fra Vittorio had even attempted to liberate himself and some inmates from the fort by means of sorcery.

Photo – Department of Information.

Plate XX

Early seventeenth-century portrait of a Hospitaller (dated 1633). The painting includes the coat-of arms of the Cassar family (top left corner). The two Cassar brothers, Vittorio and Gabriele, were in fact members of the Order. Could it be that this portrait represents the younger brother Gabriele? He was surely middle-aged by 1633.

Photo – Melitensia Art Gallery.

Plate XXI

Model of the Order's bakery in Valletta. Fra Vittorio Cassar, accompanied by his younger brother Gabriele, visited the Order's bakery in order to examine the newly-installed mill. There he discussed topics related to science and engineering with the Sicilian inventor of the mechanism.

Inquisitor's Palace, Vittoriosa. Photo – Noel Buttigieg.

Plate XXII

Aerial view of the city of Mdina. In the late-Middle Ages, Mdina was the site of a thriving Jewish community whose members were expelled from Malta in 1493. The early modern inhabitants of Mdina believed that the expelled Jews had left hidden treasures scattered all over the island.

Photo – Department of Information.

Plate XXIII

Water-colour of Garzes Tower, Mġarr (Gozo). Vittorio Cassar built
the Garzes Tower commissioned by Grand Master Martino Garzes
(1595-1601). The tower was demolished by the British in the nineteenth century. Water-colour by Salvino Busuttil.

Photo – Museum of Fine Arts, Valletta.

Plate XXIV

Coat-of-Arms of Inquisitor Evangelista Carbonese (1608-1614). Soon after the death of Vittorio Cassar, Inquisitor Carbonese heard evidence in which Cassar was described 'as knowledgeable as a demon'.

Chancery of the Inquisitor's Palace, Vittoriosa. Photo – Department of Information.

Plate XXV

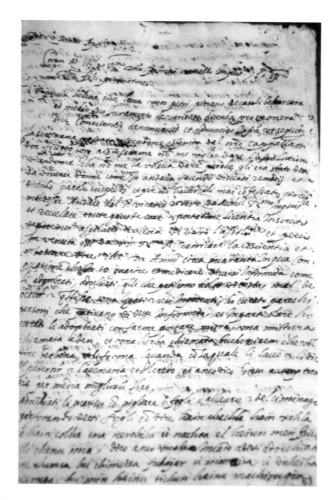

AIM Proc Crim 20 fol. 63 (1602). Luna Periano of Birkirkara, a notorious witch, explains how she practises healing spells. The text includes a couple of incantations in Maltese verse.

Cathedral Archives, Mdina. Photo – Noel Buttigieg.

Plate XXVI

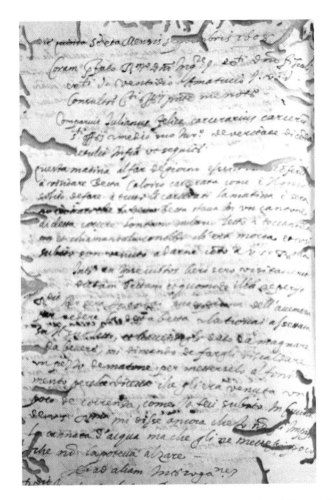

AIM Proc Crim 28C fol. 1237v. (1608). The death of Betta Caloiro at the Inquisition Prison is reported by Giuliano Felice, Prison warden of the Holy Office.

Cathedral Archives, Mdina. Photo – Noel Buttigieg.

Plate XXVII

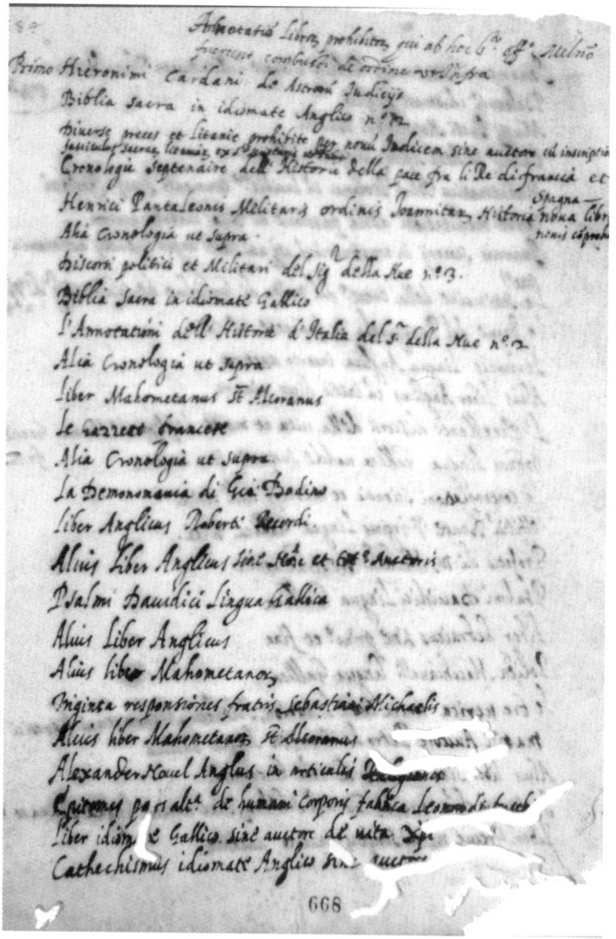

AIM Proc Crim 34B fol. 668. Front page of a list of prohibited books burned at the main square of Vittoriosa in May 1609.

Cathedral Archives, Mdina. Photo – Noel Buttigieg.

Plate XXVIII

AIM Proc Crim 26A fol. 280. The divination table originally belonging to Vittorio Cassar. It was confiscated by the Inquisition and produced as evidence against Cassar in a case on sorcery.

Cathedral Archives, Mdina. Photo – Noel Buttigieg.

Plate XXIX

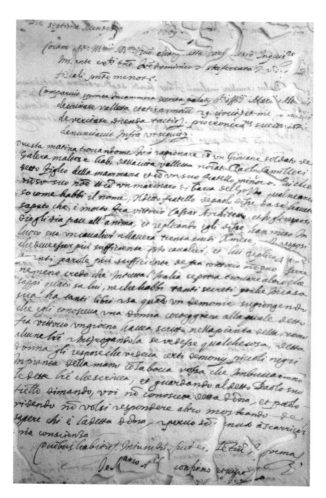

AIM Proc Crim 33A fol. 82 (1609). The death of Vittorio Cassar on 6 August 1609 was a subject much gossiped about in the harbour area. Cassar was considered to be a man of great learning.

Cathedral Archives, Mdina. Photo – Noel Buttigieg.

Plate XXX

Church of St Barbara, Gozo Citadel, with Vittorio Cassar's tombstone on the left.

Photo – Anthony P. Vella.

Plate XXXI

Tombstone of Vittorio Cassar, Gozo Citadel. Although Vittorio Cassar died in Valletta his tombstone was erected in the Gozo Citadel.

Photo – Anthony P. Vella.

Plate XXXII

to protect oneself from aggression, predict the future and acquire wealth or love'.[63] The belief in sympathetic magic and the occult versions of charms and incantations had their popular variations. So, if the *magara* recited incantations to heal the sick, the necromancer made use of the printed word which had power to control the disease.

Thus on 25 February 1608, the Gozitan priest Mattheo Zahra denounced Fra Vittorio of exorcising a Maltese woman from Żebbug in the Church of St John at the Gozo Castle. On this occasion, Fra Vittorio used a small hand-written black book which Don Mattheo assumed to be *il flagellum ò fustis Demonum*. Both Don Mattheo and Mastro Vincentio Liftech asserted that Fra Vittorio invoked the devils whom he commanded to leave the poor woman. Meanwhile, he ordered the woman to go back and forth on her knees from the door of the church to the altar, pulling her hair all the time while ordering the evil spirit to leave her body. Members of the clergy, like Don Mattheo, were obviously furious at such activities since exorcism was the realm of clerics, even though as Mastro Liftech asserted, besides being a member of the Order of St John, Fra Vittorio was also a cleric of the first tonsure.[64] Magical practices offered men and women a ritual way of dealing with crisis situations which complemented, rather than competed against, the role of the Church in society, relying as it did on the sacred for its efficacy.

Learned magic, was an entirely male phenomenon (clerical and lay), with women as passive observers, although it too made use of the realm of the sacred by frequently employing priests to conduct the intricate ceremonies. It was a well-articulated cosmology which competed against the monoploy of official religion. When applied at the local level, it did not attempt to confront the existential crises with which popular magic frequently dealt. It concerned itself with the location of buried wealth, protection from bullets and its own type of love charisma, besides satisfying the needs of those who employed it.[65]

---

[63] J.M. Sallman, *Chercheurs de Trésors et Jeteuses de Sorts*, p.186, cf. D. Gentilcore, *From Bishop to Witch*, p.226.

[64] AIM Proc Crim. 28B, case 196, fols. 826-35.

[65] C. Cassar, 'Witchcraft beliefs and social control', pp.316-30.

It is evident that the common folk were strongly attracted to the magical resources of literacy and they often used writing to communicate with supernatural forces, "unofficially", without going through the proper ecclesiastical channels. No wonder that soon after the death of Fra Vittorio Cassar on 7 August 1609, Gioanne Camilleri, referring to the knight who had replaced Fra Vittorio Cassar, asserted

> *piu sufficiente de Fra Vittorio non puo essere nemeno credo che in tutta l'Italia se potra trovare altro che sappi quanto sa lui, ne che habbi tanti secreti poiche In casa sua ha tanti libri e sa quanto un demonio...*[66]

Thus learned magic left a great impact on popular magic at both town and village level in Malta, despite the Church's firm opposition to both forms.

Ironically, popular magic, with no texts and comprehensive philosophical system, was to outlive its learned counterpart, surviving into the present day. The relation of popular magic, especially sorcery, to diabolical witchcraft has proved equally unshakeable.

---

[66] 'there could not be any better than Fra Vittorio and I do not believe that one could find anyone in Italy who is as learned as him, nor even one who knows so many secrets since at his home he keeps many books and knows as much as a devil'. AIM Proc Crim, 33A, case 285, fol.82: 7 August 1609. Text reproduced in Appendix IIIB.

Concluding Remarks

Sorcery, rather than witchcraft, seems to have been the primary concern to both lay and ecclesiastical authorities of the early modern period. Indeed witches, whether they practised beneficient or maleficient magic, continued to be denounced well into the eighteenth century.[1] In part, the attitudes of the educated strata of the clergy – from whose ranks most judges and the prosecutors were chosen – were slowly undergoing change on such issues. Not that they now denied the possibility of witchcraft: it was more a case of the increasing impossibility of establishing proof beyond doubt in particular instances. At the popular level, belief in sorcery continued much as before. And if belief in witches and the Satanic pact managed to filter down and affect notions of malefice, it had no means of expression, for the courts were increasingly reluctant to take such accusations seriously.

It seems that in early modern Malta, witchcraft accusations did not provide the enigma that they did in other European countries. The close relationship of witchcraft to *maleficium* is clear as is the role of inquisitors and demonologists in gradually diabolizing aspects of popular belief, but lacking the impact made in northern Europe. Very often, when the devil makes an appearance, it is not as a personification of evil but would show as a trickster or fairy. The devil may also appear as a bestower of favours, where the ambivalence between good and evil sources of power becomes very apparent.

This explains why an invocation to the devil was often followed by that of a saint, or by making the sign of the cross. It was such traditional beliefs and practices that the post-Tridentine Church sought to counter and define.

---

[1] F. Ciappara, 'Lay healers and sorcerers', pp. 60-76; J. Debono, 'Heresy and the Inquisition in a Frontier Society,' ch.1; A. Camenzuli, 'Inquisition and Society in Mid-Eighteeneth Century Malta', ch.2.

The case-studies developed in the foregoing chapters are evidence that at the dawn of the seventeenth century, religion served as a response to the existential needs of an essentially agrarian society. It provided protection against the vagaries of the weather, the irruption of disease into everyday life, and other misfortunes that were constantly threatening the order which man attempted to impose on the cosmos. For this reason the most fundamental components were those rituals meant to respond to the 'extraordinary' by addressing the power of the supernatural. The sacraments of the Catholic Church were undoubtedly important, for these too rendered possible access to the sacred, especially those relating to the biological rites of passage. The rituals of baptism and annointing of the sick were accompanied by popular twists and interpretations. But the rituals that most fitted the everyday needs of the faithful were of a more *ad hoc* spontaneous kind, be they of ecclesiastical or folkloric origin. Thus Church sacramentals and ecclesiastical 'medicines' – prayer, rosary, pilgrimage, procession, blessing, exorcism, and other – mingled with popular beliefs, invocations and ritual cures.

'Official' and 'popular' religion interacted and borrowed from each another. It is therefore, often difficult to clearly distinguish between what is 'official' and what is of 'popular' origin. In terms of participation, everyone belonged to and utilized the orthodox rites of the Church though not necessarily to the same degree (i.e. prostitutes often went to church and so did sorceresses). At the same time, many clerics made use of lay and popular rituals, generally condemned by the Church hierarchy as 'superstitious'. When someone was taken ill, a presumed victim of a neighbour's sorcery, that patient could seek confirmation of the malady's origin and a cure through a pool of ritual remedies, some clerical and some lay, pragmatically trying one, then another, until hopefully the necessary cure was obtained. Often what determined the type of 'healer' consulted – wise woman, priest, exorcist, physician – was a question of availability, accessibility and reputation, despite the Church's attempts to convince the people that it was equipped to deal with diseases of maleficial origin.

Despite frequent preaching, the notion of Satan as all-evil and the cause of sin in the world – propagated by the Council of Trent – was slow to take root. Evidence from the archives, particularly the depositions to the Inquisition in witchcraft cases, indicate that the devil continued to be interpreted as the trickster of folklore well into the eighteenth century. From the early modern period onwards, this view of the devil was largely relegated to popular culture as practised by the lower echelons of society. Such a notion remained evidently strong even in the nineteenth and early twentieth centuries.[2] One may conclude that the Tridentine Church was at least partially successful in diabolising the notion of unethical behaviour.

Nonetheless, both the popular and learned forms of magic continued to overlap at the practical level. This happened because learned magic was interested in practical applications like exorcism, love and protective magic, and particularly treasure-hunting, rather than philosophical speculations. The 'learned' magic practised by the necromancers included the use of written spells. These formulae had the same impact as the magical powers utilized by witches in their attempt to control a hostile environment and in explaining misfortune and all sorts of failures. In fact, the ambivalence of the demonic in the rest of early modern Malta – as in southern Catholic Europe – is most clearly expressed in the local versions of witchcraft and the satanic pact, which were never completely diabolized.[3] Indeed they lack the evil, community-threatening element expressed in other regions of Europe.

The evidence discussed above suggests that oral and literate cultures not only coexisted, but, at times, they also interacted. Still popular healing rituals, the evil eye and other related forms of witchcraft, essentially formed part of the female domain, in line with the woman's role in caring for the well-being of the domestic group. On the other hand, learned magic was exclusively male, and

---

[2] G. Pitrè, *Usi e Costumi*, Vol.4. pp.72-109. In Maltese idiom, the devil *xitan* is associated with trouble. Thus the idioms: *ix-xitan m'ghandux halib, ghad li jaghmel il-ġbejniet* (Trouble ensues when there is no need to create it) and *ix-xitan deffes denbu* for when trouble ensues for no apparent reason. K. Fenech, *Idjomi Maltin*, p.101.

[3] 'One of the most striking features of Italian and Spanish witchcraft prosecutions was the rarity of charges of collective Devil-worship... in the large majority of cases heard by the Spanish and Roman inquisitors, especially in the southern parts of both peninsulas, these charges are completely absent. Peasants and town dwellers were accused of performing various types of magic, and their magic was viewed as heretical, but it was thought of much more as pagan superstition than as diabolical apostasy'. B.P. Levack, *The Witch-hunt in Early Modern Europe*, pp.201-202.

involved any layman or cleric who had a good knowledge of reading and writing. On its part the Church was caught in what P. Burke calls 'a classic double bind, with a problem if it encouraged the spread of literacy, and another one if it did not'.[4]

In this study, I have attempted to describe a more or less constant social structure. However it does not mean that it was immobile. New forms of devotion were periodically introduced, gained favour and took their place alongside more traditional ritual forms. On the other hand, the Tridentine reforms of the Church aimed at eradicating, or christianising, what it defined as 'superstitious' or unorthodox. This had the least impact on the mass of society. As the basic structures, from agricultural techniques to standards of life, remained basically unchanged during the early modern period, there was no shift away from traditionally held notions of the supernatural. Nor was there a radical shift in social attitudes, expectations and behaviour. Finally there was little difference between town and country religiosity, perhaps due to the fact that agricultural structures filtered and dominated even city-culture. As far as early modern Malta is concerned, there were hardly any noticeable changes in the religious attitudes of the ordinary folk. What characterizes the model is continuity; for until relatively recent years, most of the population continued to participate actively in religious ceremonies and believed in the power of religious symbolism whether it offered the comforts of the sacramentals or that of witchcraft.

---

[4] P. Burke, *The Historical Anthropology of Early Modern Italy*, p.123.

Appendix I

Case referring to the death of Betta Caloiro at the Prisons of the Inquisition in Vittoriosa on 6 September 1608

Die sexta mensis septembris 1608

Coram prefato Reverendissimo domino Inquisitore examinati domino fiscali domino ventidio Amatucio J.U.D. Consultorem Sancti Offitii presente me notario

In the presence of His Most Reverend the Inquisitor, and the inquiring officer, the fiscal master Ventidio Amatuccio JUD, advisor of this Holy Office, and myself as notary.

Comparuit Julianus Felice carcerarius carcerum Sancti Offitii e medio suo juramento de veritate dicenda retulit infra ut sequitur

Giuliano Felice, prison warden of the Holy Office, took an oath that he would say the truth, and he stated the following

Questa matina al far del giorno essendome conferito à visitare Betta Caloiro carcerata come il mio solito de fare à tutti li carcerati la matina sera ho trovato che la detta Betta stava in un cantone di detta carcere lontana dal suo letto e toccandola et chiamandola conobbi ch'era morta et cosi subito son venuto a darne conto a Vostra Signoria Reverendissima

This morning at sunrise, I went to visit the prisoner Betta Caloiro, as I am used to do to all the prisoners every morning and evening. Betta was in a corner of the cell far away from her bed and on touching and calling her I realized that she was dead and so I immediately came to inform your Most Reverend Lordship

Interrogatus an ipse custos heri sero visitaverit dictam Bettam et quo modo illam reperiit

Asked whether as prison warden, the previous evening, he visited the said Betta and what was her health condition.

Respondit: hier sera Io andai puoco prima dell'Ave Maria per vedere la detta Betta e la trovai assettata su il suo letto, e havendogli dato da magnare e da bevere, mi dimando de fargli riscaldare un pezzo de matone per metterselo al fondamento perrche diceva che gli era venuta un poco de correnza, come Io feci subito In cucina de Vostra Signoria Reverendissima mi disse ancora che Io non gli la cannata d'acqua ma che gli ne mettessi poco perche non la poteva alzare

Replied: Yesterday evening, a little before the ringing of the first Ave Maria, I went to visit Betta and found her sitting on her bed. On giving her food and drink, she asked me to warm a piece of brick to heat her bed since she was feeling sick. I immediately went to your Reverend lordship's kitchen to accommodate her. She then told me not to fill her water jug to the brim but to pour a little water because she could not lift it up.

Et ad aliam interrogationem

And his reply to other questions.

Respondit: Io vedendo la detta Betta che stava con detta correnza dubitar che sendo cosi vechia non morisse gli dimandai se voleva confessarse al padre Maestro Damiano conforme il solito suo, et ella mi rispose si si, et io stavo con intento de chiamare detto padre per sentire la sua confessione come fece altre volte

As soon as I noticed that Betta was sick I thought that she might die due to her old age. Therefore I asked her whether she wanted to confess to (the Dominican) Father Damiano (Taliana) as she did often. She answered yes, yes, and I left with the intention of calling the friar to hear her confession as he did on other occasions.

Interrogatus quare illicum non indicavit predicta omnia Reverendissimi domino cum ipse met fateate severi de morte ipsius ad hoc ut potuisset consuli saluti eius anime, et hoc saltem facere debeat (...) consignatione clavium vespertinis horis ut (m...)

Asked why he did not report the matter to the Most Reverend Inquisitor when he confessed that she was on the point of death and so she would have found comfort for her soul. The least he could have done at the time he returned the keys in the evening.

Respondit: Monsignore io non pensai che la detta Betta dovesse morire cosi subito per un puoco de correnza maggiormente che il solito suo era de stare assettata nel letto, e la ritrovai con la medesima voce che soleva parlare

Replied: Monsignor I did not realize that Betta could die so quick-ly, due to a little sickness, particularly since she often stayed sitting on her bed, and I found her speaking to herself as usual

Interrogatus an ipse sciat officium custodis carcerari que ad ipsum spectat

Asked whether he knew his duties as prison warden.

Respondit: Signor si Io so che l'officio del; carceriere de visitare sera matina li carcerati per vedere quello gli fa bisogno et Io non ho detto altro a Vostra Signoria Reverendissima della detta Betta perche non pensavo che dovesse morire cosi presto

Yes sir, I know that the prison warden is supposed to visit the prisoners evening and morning and see to their needs but I did not inform your Most Reverend Lordship on Betta because I did not realize that she could die so soon.

Etiam aliam opportunam interrogationes

To other relevant questions.

Respondit: Io ho viosto piu volte a Vostra Signoria Reverendissima tanto di giorno come di notte venire à vedere la detta Betta et in particolare mi ricordo ch'una sera venne lei in compagnia del Signor Gio. Domenico Vella assessore et il suo auditore et essorto detta Betta in presenza mia a partirse di suoi errori e dimandarne perdono al Signor Iddio dandogli una crucetta benedetta quali lei prese bagiandola e se la mese al collo, mormorando segno di contritione, anzi l'ho vista piu volte digiunare quando vennere, quando il sabbato et altri giorni di vigilia e di quattro tempore

Replied: I have noticed that many a time, both at daytime and night-time, your Most Reve-rend Lordship came to visit Betta. On one occasion you were accompanied by the assessor, Signor Gio Domenico Vella, and the uditore. In my presence you exhorted Betta to give up her errors and ask the Lord God for his pardon. You also gave her a small blessed crucifix which she took in her hands, kissed it and put it round her neck, murmuring words of repentance. Indeed I have often noticed her fasting on Friday or Saturday and other days of penance and during Lent

Tunc dominus acceptatis avessit una cum dictis dominus ad di dictas carceres e invenit eamdem Betta prostratam seus eius cubile in parte ipsius carceris mortuam, propea dominus mandavit accersiri examinatem Nicolaus Ciliam Phisicum ad effectum illam ispiciendi qua morte fuit preventa

The Inquisitor having approved of this answer, came to the prisons and found the corpse of Betta on her bed. Then he order that the physician Nicola Cilia be summoned to make a post mortem examination and establish the cause of her death.

Interrogatus medicus postque visitavit e inspexerit cadaver presente Betta e medio suo juramento retulit per modum ut sequitur vz:

On being asked, the physician, after an examination of the corpse of the said Betta, swore the following:

Monsignor Reverendissimo secondo il, mio parere e giudicio dico che questa Betta sia morta per piu cause cio trovandosi in eta decrepita havendo havuto doi o tre mesi di carceressendogli sopravenuto un flusso di ventre per quanto referse il custode delle carceri ha hier sera inqua, havendola ritrovata cosi decrepita et debile giudico che con ogni celerita resto priva della vita

Most Reverend Monsignor, according to my judgement and opinion I must say that Betta has passed away due to several causes. In the first place she was very old; furthermore she spent two or three months in prison, and since yesterday evening, and according to the prison warden, she has been having a blood discharge from her breast [tuberculosis?]. Her weakness and old age led to her death

Io Nicola Cilia medico

Eodem Die sexta mensis septembris 1608

Cadaver supradictae Betta Caloirem iuxta votum congregationis emanatum sub die hodierna fuit repositum intus ipsum seu arcam signeam noviter astructam et crucem e ibea de super signatam, et loco depositi inhumatum intus viridariolum Sancti Offitii usque ad expeditionem cause et novum ordinem sacre congregationis Alme vobis unde

On agreement among members of the Congregation, the corpse of Betta Caloiro has been buried at the Palace of the Holy Office and a cross indicates where it is resting. This was done until further orders from the Sacred Congregation were issued

[AIM Proc Crim Vol 28C case 227
fols. 1237v-1238v : 6 September 1608]

Appendix II

List of Books Burned at the Main Square of Vittoriosa by order of Inquisitor Evangelista Carbonese on 5 May 1609

Adnotatio librorum prohibitorum qui ab hoc Sancto Offitio Melivetano fuerunt combusti de ordine ut infra
Et Primo Hieronimi Cardani de Astrorum Judiciis

Biblia Sacra in idiomate Anglico no. 2

Diverse preces et litanie prohibite per novum Judicem sine auctore cum inscriptione fasciculus sacrarum litaniarum ex Sanctis Scripturis et pribus

Cronologia septenaire dell'Historia della pace fra li Re di Francia et Spagna

Henrici Pantaleonis Militaris ordinis Joannitarum Historia nova libris nonis comprehens

Alia cronologia ut supra

Discorsi politici et Militari del Signor della Nue no. 3

Biblia Sacra in idiomate Gallico

L'Annotationi dell'Historie d'Italia del Signor della Nue no. 2

Alia Cronologia ut supra

Liber Mahometanus st Alcoranus

Le Gazzette francese

Alia Cronologia ut supra

La Demonomania di Gianni Bodino

Liber Anglicus Roberti Recordi

Alius liber Anglicus sine nomen et sine auctoris

Psalmi Davidici Lingua Gallica

Alius Liber Anglicus

Alius liber Mahometanorum

Triginta responsiones fratris Sebastiani Michaelis

Alius liber Mahometanorum st Alcoranus

Alexander Novel Anglus in articulis Rabg..nx

Epitomus pa alt.a de humani corporis fabrica Leonardi (Fusch ?)

Liber idiomate Gallico sine auctore de vita Christi

Catechismus idiomate Anglico sine auctore

Inventarium Historiarum Gallia idiomate Gallico auctore Theande Serres no.2 alia quinque Joannis de Serres

Psalterium idiomate Anglico

Mutii Justi Nopolitani Duellum

Evangelia et Acta Apostolorum idiomate Gallico no. 2

Mathematica Divi Ptolomei cum Lucidissimo comento Hieronimo Cardani

Certe mediationi della passione di Christo incerto auctore

Joannis Sconerii in constructione atque usum recti anguli sive radii astronomici annotates

Le settimaine della creazione del mondo di Guglielmo de Saluste Signore d'Ubartas no. 8

Le dogme del Panigarola in francese no.2

Sermones Lingua Anglica incerto auctore

Alius Liber Anglicus cum initio disce vivere

L'Eccellenti discorsi della vita et morte de filippo de Mornai Gentilhomo francese

Orationes Lingua Gallica valde suspecte sine auctore

Le contemplationi scientie et misterii dell'Asini

Offitium Beate Virginis Lingua Gallica no. 2

Profetie de mastri Michele Nostradamos

Psalmi Davidici Lingua Gallica

Liber hebraicus sine principio et fine

Politica Macchiavelli lingua Gallica

Le tre verita contro tutti L'Atteisti, Idolatri, Mahometani, heretici et schismatici Auctore Petro Le Carron Lingua Gallica

Alius libri sine auctore de romano benevivendi

Institutio christiane pietatis as usum scholarum sine auctore lingua Latina et Greca

Liber Grecus manu scriptis incerto auctore

L'opere di mastro francesco Rabellais Dottor in medicine Lingua Gallica

Basilicodoron Lingua Gallica

L'hore di nosrta Signora Lingua Hispana

Liber Arabicus reputatus Alcoranus

Preces Mahometanorum

Die quarta mensis Maii 1609. Demandato Ad: Illustrissimis et Reverendissimi domini Evangeliste Carbonesii Inquisitoris Instante executi domino Joanne dominico Testaferrata J.U.D. promotore fiscali Sancti Offitii omnes suprascripti libri fuerunt conbusti In publica plathea Civitatis Victoriose multitudine populi Ibidem astante, presentibus dicto domino fiscali, Domino Valerio Miccio J.U.D. e Magnifico Martino Vella Capitaneo ac me notario, et pro testibus Reverendo Domino Don Petro de franchis, Josepho burlo, Antonio fiteni, et Aloisio Pace e aliis[1]

     Ita est Notarius Joannes Lucas Gaucius
     Sancti offitii Magister notarius demanus

[AIM Proc Crim Vol 34B case 584, fols 668-69]

---

[1] 4 May 1609. Illustrious Reverend Inquisitor Evangelista Carbonese ordered the Fiscal (Public Prosecutor) of the Holy Office, Domino Joan Domenico Testaferrata, to burn the above books in the public square of Vittoriosa in the presence of a multitude of people. There were also present the Domino fiscale, the Domino Valerio Miccio J.U.D. (judge), Magnifico Martino Vella Captain of the Inquisition and myself as notary. The witnesses were Reverend Domino Don Petro de Franchis, Josepho Burlo, Antonio Fiteni, Aloisio Pace, and others. Notary Joan Luca Gauci Master Notary of the Holy Office

Appendix IIIA

Evidence given by the Sicilian Mariano De Adriano on the magical activities of Fra Vittorio Cassar

Die xxii Januarii 1609

Coram Illustrissimo Reverendissimo Domino Evangelista Carbonesio Inquisitore assistente examinati domino Valerio Micci J.U.D. et instante examinati domino Joanne Domenico Testaferrata J.U.D. promotore fiscali presente me notaro.

In the presence of His Eminence and Most Reverend Evangelista Carbonese, the Inquisitor, assisted by the inquiring officers Valerio Micci JUD and Giovanni Domenico Testaferrata JUD, fiscal master and myself as notary.

Comparuit sponte in cammera secreta palatii Sancti Officii Marianus De Adriano siculus Castri Joannis etatis annorum 30 circiter et medio suo juramento de veritate dicenda tactis pro exoneratione sue coscientie denunciavit Infra ut sequitur

Spontaneous comparition at the tribunal room, in the palace of the Holy Office, of the Sicilian Mariano De Adriano from the town of Castro Giovanni (Enna), aged about thirty, and after taking an oath reported the following.

Da novi mesi in qua trovandome Io nell'Isola del Gozzo à servire per scrivano nella fabrica che si fa li al forte della marina et con tal occasione ho havuto amicicia intrinsica et familiarita con Fra Vittorio Cassar Architetto di detta fabrica, et piu volte raggionando insieme de molte cose mi hebbe a dire come lui sa fare gran cose et sa molti secreti, et in particolare mi disse che è sufficiente negromante, et magaro et che tratta con i demoni e spiriti a modo suo e da essi puo sapere quando vole

I have served as clerk of the works which are being carried out at the Gozo harbour for the last nine months. During this time I befriended Fra Vittorio Cassar, the engineer-in-charge of the project. In our discussion of several subjects he often referred to his knowledge of many secrets, and particularly to his ability as necromancer and wizard. He stated that he can deal with demons and spirits from whom he usually gets to know whatever he wants. He also told me that he has been

tutto quello desiderami disse come altre
volte è stato inquisito in questo Santo
Officio suggiongendome che havendo egli
non so che libri de negromancia et de
magaria in casa d'una donna corteggiana
siciliana de siragusa che stava questi di
passati di casa in rincontro della casa del
Signor Fra Agostino Tabone alla citta
Valletta e havendo presentimento esso Fra
Vittorio che la detta donna dovea essere
cercata dal Santo Officio la fece andar via a
Napoli dove non potendosi fermare ritor-
nata qui in salvo, mi disse anco questi
giorni passati come havea havuto haviso di
qua di Malta come il Santo Officio voleva
fargli perquisitione nelle sue stanze per
trovargli libri prohibiti e questi libri che
tiene de negromancia e magaria e che
perciò havea nascosto detti libri in luoco che
mai se sarebbono trovati ma che lui se ne
serviva d'essi comodamente quando voleva.

questioned several times by
the Holy Office. He added that
he was owner of several books
on necromancy and witchcraft
which he kept in the house of
a Sicilian courtesan from
Syracuse. This house is adja-
cent to the house of Fra
Agostino Tabone in Valletta.
He got to know that this
woman's house was about to
be searched by the Holy
Office, but Fra Vittorio
managed to send her to
Naples from where she
returned to Malta some time
later. He also got to know that
the Holy Office intended to
carry out a search for prohibited books on necromancy and
witchcraft in his rooms. Thus
he hid these books in a place
where they could not be
found, while at the same time,
he could keep on using them.

Di piu questi di mi disse che doi messinesi
amici suoi quali erano stati seco al Gozzo
doppo erano partiti doveano ritornare à
trovarlo quanto prima perche gia li voleva
insegnare l'arte de negromancia, e havendogli io resposto che stimavo che non ci
retorneranno et egli mi replicò si si che
torneranno e lo so dalli spiriti che mi han
riferito che sensa fallo veneranno, et di
queste cose ragionassemo cos qui a Malta
come al Gozzo.

Furthermore he told me that
two friends of his from
Messina, who had spent some
time with him in Gozo, will
soon return to Malta because
he had to teach them the art
of necromancy. When De
Adriano expressed a negative
opinion Fra Vittorio replied
that they will come back since
the spirits had assured him
that they will return. We
spoke of these matters both in
Malta and in Gozo.

M'occorre dire ancora che un Agostino Borg
guardiano di detta fabrica questi di passati
mi disse come lui sapeva che detto Fra
Vittorio Cassar è gran magaro e che parla
con li spiriti con mettere un puoco d'
inchiostro alla pianta della mano d'un figlio
lo vergine e dicendo certe parole fa venire li

I must also say that Agostino
Borg, the warden in charge of
the building site, recently
assured me that Fra Vittorio
Cassar is a great wizard who
communicates with the spirits
by putting some ink on the
palm of the hand of a virgin
child and mumbles a few
words and gets whatever he

spiriti, et con mezzo di detto vergine sa detti spiriti tutto quello desidera, et io volevo dire à detto Agostino ch' cosa del Santo Officio ma perche gran amico di detto Fra Vittorio percio non gli ho volsuto dire altro.

wants. I wanted to tell Agostino that the Holy Office should be informed of this but since he is a very close friend of Fra Vittorio I did not want to tell him anything else.

Di piu il detto Fra Vittorio mi disse che lui sa stringere li spiriti à modo suo in un anello, ò altra cosa per poter servirse per farlo vincere al gioco, ò per altra occasione et facendo io de tutte queste cose scrupolo ho volsuto venire a scarricare mia conscienza in questo Santo Officio.

Furthermore the said Fra Vittorio told me that he could control the spirits by using a ring or other items which could make him win at games, or for other reasons. I came here to the Holy Office in order to put my conscience at rest.

Interrogatus: quenam alia persone sint informate de praemissis.

Asked: How many others knew about the matter

Respondit: tutte queste cose e raggiona-menti passarno da me in lui, ma facilmente puo esser informato il prete della Mellecha perche ha gran familiarita della detta donna siracusana la quale qualche volta va da detto prete passando al Gozzo et ci va da lui a spasso sola.

Replied: All these discussions passed between me and him, but it is possible that the rector of the Mellieħa sanc-tuary may know something else since the Syracuse woman is very close to him. She frequently stops at the church on her way to Gozo since she often travels alone.

Interrogatus: an ira odio inimicicia inter vel alia animi passe praemissa deposuerit.

Asked: Whether he denounced his true anger, hate, hostility or any other passion.

Respondit: quello Io ho revelato qui l'ho detto per scarrico di mia conscienza sensa passione alcuna, anzi detto Fra Vittorio mi amico e amicissimo e non mezza hora che eramo insieme alla citta Valletta in casa sua et mi dispiace del suo mal governo.

Replied: Whatever I have re-vealed here I was said to re-lieve my conscience without any passion whatsoever. Rather the said Fra Vittorio is a very good friend of mine to the extent that I was with him at his house in Valletta about half an hour ago and I am sorry for his misdeeds.

Interrogatus: quare tam diu distulerit denunciare praemissa.

Asked: Why did he take so long to denounce all this.

Respondit: non son venuto perche queste cose gravi non l'intesi da lui e da detto Agostino solamente da venti giorni in qua,

Replied: I did not come before because I only learned all these matters from himself and Agostino in the last twenty days

ma per prima mi diceva qualche cosa leggiera et io son sempre stato si come son travagliato non me son curato di venire. *Quibus habitis et iunctum fuit ei silentium in forma e fuit ad cauthelam per dominum absolutus informa.*

or so. Previously he used to say little about these things and since I am always at work it was not possible to come here.

Whereupon he was obliged not to divulge anything publicly and was thus absolved for security's sake

Io Mariano Deandriano confirmo ut supra

[AIM Proc Crim Vol 28B case 197 fols.843-44]

Appendix IIIB

Case referring to the death of Fra Gio Vittorio Cassar, Architect Civil Engineer and Necromancer on 6 August 1609

Die septima Mensis Augusti 1609

Coram Ad:
Illustrissimo et Reverendissimo Domino Evangelista Carbonesio Inquisitore Instante examinati domino Joanne dominico Testaferrata J.U.D. promotore fiscali presente me notario

In the presence of His Eminence and Most Reverend Evangelista Carbonese, the Inquisitor, and the inquiring offiver Giovanni Domenico Testaferrata JUD, fiscal master and myself as notary.

Comparuit sponte In cammera secreta palatii Sancti Offitii Marius Albanus de civitate Valletta etatis annorum 29 circiter et me de veritate dicenda tactis pro exoneratione sue coscientie denuncia vit Infra ut sequitur

Spontaneous comparition at the tribunal room, in the palace of the Holy Office, of Mario Albano from Valletta, aged about twenty nine, and after taking an oath he reported the following.

Questa matina trovandome Io a ragionare con un giovane soldato de Galera maltese habitante della citta Valletta nominato Paolo Camilleri detto figlio della mammana et con un suo fratello minor di lui che non so suo nome et con un marinaro di barca del Gozzo qual neanco so come habbi il

This morning I was talking to Paolo Camilleri, called son of the midwife, a young Maltese galley soldier who lives in Valletta, his younger brother whose name I do not know, and a sailor of the Gozo boat whom I do not know by name either. Paolo's brother said,

nome, Il detto fratello de paolo disse da se havete saputo che morto Fra Vittorio Cassar Architetto, et io gli resposi dio gli dia pace all'anima, et replican do egli disse han meso In luoco suo un cavaliere e havera trenta scudi Il mese, io gli resposi che deve esser più che sufficiente questo cavaliere, et lui replico questi seguenti parole pi sufficiente de Fra Vittorio non puo essere ne meno credo che In tutta l'Italia se potra trovare altro che sappi quanto sa lui, ne che habbi tanti secreti poiche In casa sua ha tanti libri e sa quanto un demonio, sugiongendo che egli conosceva una donna corteggiana alla quale detto Fra Vittorio un giorno havea scritto nella pianta della mano alcune lettere e Interrogandola se ve desse qualche cosa, detta donna gli respose che vedeva certi demoni piccoli negri In pianta della mano con la bocca rossa che Imbuccavano le dette lettere che scrivea, et guardando al detto Paolo suo fratello dimando, voi non conoscete detta donna, et paolo ridendo non volse respondere altro mostrando de sapere chi la detta donna, e percio son venuto à scarricare mia conscienza

'Did you hear of the death of the architect Fra Vittorio Cassar?', and I answered, 'May his soul rest in peace'. And the young man continued, 'He has been replaced by another knight who will get an income of thirty scudi per month'. Paolo's brother then continued, 'He can never be more sufficient then Fra Vittorio nor do I believe that in all of Italy one could find anyone as learned as Fra Vittorio, nor one that knows so many secrets because he has so many books at home and he is as knowledgeable as a demon. He further added that he knew a courtesan to whom Fra Vittorio wrote some letters on the palm of her hand. When he asked her some questions the woman said that she could see several small black demons on the palm of her hand. The demons had red mouths and swallowed the letters which Fra Vittorio was writing. At this point the young man asked his brother Paolo 'Do you know this woman?' Paolo started laughing and would not answer showing that he knew this woman and thus I came here to relieve my conscience.

Quibus habitis.

Iniunctium fuit ei silentium in forma

Whereupon he was obliged not to divulge anything publicly

Io Marco Albano confirmo ut supra

Die viii.a idem mensis Augusti

Coram prefacto Illustrissimo Inquisitore Instante examinati domino fisci promotore presente me notario

In the presence of His Eminence the Inquisitor, and the inquiring officer, the fiscal master and myself as notary.

Paulus Camilleri melitense filius bendi de civitate Valletta etatis annorum triginta circiter bombarderius salariatus sacre Religionis Hierosolimitane testis vocatus

Paolo Camilleri, Maltese, son of Bendo of Valletta, aged about thirty, salaried gunner with the Order's galleys, called to witness, who on

delato sibi Juramento de veritate dicenda tactis es.

taking the oath stated

Interrogatus an sciat cam suae vocationis vel saltem illam suspecta

Asked: Whether he knew why he was called to testify or whether, at least, he suspected anything.

Respondit: Io non so la causa ne meno mel'imagino

Replied: I do not know the reason nor could I recall anything.

Interrogatus an a duobus diebus diebus audiverit aliquod dui ab aliquo spectans as hoc Sanctus officium e quid.

Asked: Whether within the last two days he had heard anything which was relevant to this Holy Office.

Respondit: Io mi recordo che hier matino mio fratello nominato Gioanne Camilleri soldato di Galera mi disse come fra vittorio Cassar era morto, suggiongendo ch'era molto curioso et Intelligente e sapeva assai, e che un giorno ha Inteso esso mio fratello che detto fra Vittorio Cassar fece un poco d'Inchiostro nella pianta della mano d'una donna e che subito fece comparire certi demoni piccoli con la bocca rossa, e dimando à me se Io sapessi della donna che fosse, e Io mi mesi à ridere pigliando la cosa In burla, altro non so d'haver Inteso

Replied: I recall that yesterday morning my brother called Gioanne Camilleri, soldier of the galleys, told me how Fra Vittorio Cassar had passed away, adding that he was very inquisitive and intelligent and that he knew a lot of things. On one occasion my brother heard that Fra Vittorio Cassar wrote certain words on the palm of the hand of a woman and some small demons with red mouths soon appeared. My brother then asked me whether I knew the said woman and I started laughing taking it as a joke, I do not know anything else.

Et Interrogatus ac monitus ad fatem veritatem ut dicat quo nam sit Ista mulier cui fuit con spurcata manus a dicto quondam fratrem victorio Cassar

Asked and warned to confess the truth and say who this woman was, on whose hands were written words by Fra Vittorio Cassar.

Respondit Io non la conosco ne so che sia, ma mio fratello disse che la conosce perche mi disse che cio Intese dalla Istessa donna qual non ha nominato

Replied: I do not know this woman, but my brother knows her because he told me what she had said but he did not mention her name.

Quibus habitis. Iniunctum fuit ei silentium In forma

Whereupon he was obliged not to divulge anything in public.

Die xii Augusti 1609
Coram prefacto Reverendissimo Domino
Inquisitore examinati domino fisci promo-
tore presente me notario

In the presence of His
Eminence the Inquisitor, and
the inquiring officer, the fiscal
master and myself as notary.

Joannes Cammilleri miles... triremus
Sancti Stephani Sacra Religione
Hieroslomitani annorum hab civitate
Valletta testis voca tus delato sibi jura-
mento de veritate dicenda

Joanne Camilleri soldier on
the Order's galley St Stephen
from Valletta, called to
witness, who took an oath
that he will say the truth

*Interrogatus an sciat cam suae vocationis
suspiciet*

Asked whether he knew why
he was called to testify or
whether, at least, he suspected
anything.

Respondit: Io non so la causa ne meno mi
l'imagino

Replied: I do not know the
reason or can I recall
anything.

Interrogatus ansciat ali quod factum
spectans ad hoc Sanctus Offitium

Asked whether he knew
anything about which the Holy
Office should be informed.

Respondit: Io non so fatto alcuno che
appartenga a questo Santo Officio

I do not know anything which
should be denounced at this
Holy Office

*Interrogatus an ... sex diebus citra dixerit
aliquod factum alicui quod pertineat ad hoc
Sanctus Officium e quod.*

Asked whether within the last
six days he became aware of
someone's misdeed which
belonged to the Holy Office.

Respondit: Io non so ne mi ricordo d'altro se
non che circa doi anni sono poco pi o meno
conferendome Io all'Isola del Gozzo su una
barca, dove vi erano due donne quali non
conosco ne so se fossero de Malta, ò del
Gozzo, che ragionavano Insieme per camino
et una de loro disse per li sequenti parole,
havete mai visto che cose se fanno, Io son
stata mandata da fra Vittorio per curarme
d'un male che patisco, et egli subito che me
vidde me pose certo Inchiostro alla pianta
della mano e subito fece comparire due cose
come fossero due chiaule i, quali han
magnato detto inchiostro, et con occasione
doppo che questa settimana passata morse

I do not recall other than the
following: Around two years
ago, while I was travelling to
Gozo on a Gozo boat, there
were two women whom I am
not sure whether they were
Maltese, or Gozitan. These
women were talking between
themselves while walking on
board and one of them said
the following words, 'Have you
heard what happened? I went
to Fra Vittorio to heal me
from a disease from which I
suffer and on looking at me he
put some ink on the palm of
my hand. Two demon like
creatures soon appeared on
my hand and started eating
the ink. Fra Vittorio has just
died in Valletta, and since I

detto fra Vittorio Cassar nella citta Valletta
Io trovandome con mio fratello Paolo
Camilleri e non so che altri gli ho narrato
quest fatto, e non sapevo veramente esser
cosa che spettava à questo Santo Officio.

was with my brother Paolo
Camilleri and others I
narrated the above case. But I
was not aware that I had to
denounce the matter at this
Holy Office'.

Quibus habitis.
Iniuncto fuit ei silentium In forma

Whereupon he was obliged not
to divulge anything in public.

[AIM Proc Crim Vol 33A case 285 fols.82-83]

Appendix IV

Inquisitors of Malta 1562-1798

Domenico Cubelles	1562-1566
Martino Royasde Portalrubeo	1572-1574
Pietro Dusina	1574-1575
Pietro Sant'Humano	1575-1577
Reynaldo Corso	1577-1579
Domenico Petrucci	1579-1580
Federico Cefalotto	1580-1583
Pietro Francesco Costa	1583-1585
Ascanio Libertano	1585-1587
Giovanni Battista Petralta	1587
Paola Bellardito	1587-1591
Angelo Gemmario	1591
Paolo Bellardito	1591-1592
Giovanni Ludovico dell'Armi	1592-1595
Innocenzo del Bufalo de' Cancellieri	1595-1598
Antonio Hortensio	1598-1600
Fabrizio Verallo	1600-1605
Ettore Diotallevi	1605-1607
Leonetto della Corbara	1607-1608
Evangelista Carbonese	1608-1614
Fabio della Lagonessa	1614-1619
Antonio Tornielli	1619-1621
Paolo Torello	1621-1623

Carlo Bovio	1623-1624
Onorato Visconti	1624-1627
Nicolò Herrera	1627-1630
Ludovico Serristori	1630-1631
Martino Alfieri	1631-1634
Fabio Chigi	1634-1639
Giovanni Battista Gori Pannellini	1639-1646
Antonio Pignatelli	1646-1649
Carlo Cavalletti	1649-1652
Federico Borromeo	1653-1655
Giulio degli Oddi	1655-1658
Gerolamo Casanate	1658-1663
Galeazzo Marescotti	1663-1666
Angelo Ranuzzi	1667-1668
Carlo Bichi	1668-1670
Giovanni Tempi	1670-1672
Ranuccio Pallavicino	1672-1676
Ercole Visconti	1677-1678
Giacomo Cantelmo	1678-1683
Innico Caracciolo	1683-1686
Tommaso Vidoni	1686-1690
Francesco Acquaviva d'Aragona	1691-1694
Tommaso Ruffo	1694-1698
Giacinto Filiberto Ferrero di Messerano	1698-1703
Giorgio Spinola	1703-1706
Giacomo Caracciolo	1706-1710
Ranieri d'Elci	1711-1715
Lazzaro Pallavicino	1718-1719
Antonio Ruffo	1720-1728
Fabrizio Serbelloni	1728-1730
Giovanni Francesco Stoppani	1731-1735
Carlo Francesco Durini	1735-1739
Ludovico Gualterio Gualtieri	1739-1743
Paolo Passionei	1743-1754
Gregorio Salviati	1754-1759
Angelo Maria Durini	1760-1766
Giovanni Ottavio Mancinforte	1767-1771
Antonio Lante	1771-1777
Antonio Felice Zondadari	1777-1785
Giovanni Filippo Gallarati Scotti	1785-1793
Giulio Carpegna	1793-1798

Bibliography

Manuscript Sources

National Library of Malta, Valletta

a. Archives of the Order of Malta:

98	Liber Conciliorum	1589-1594.
414	Liber Bullarum	1528-1530.
416	Liber Bullarum	1534-1537.
440	Liber Bullarum	1581-1582.

b. Library Manuscripts:

Vol. 23   Varia.
Vol. 643   Visitatio Apostolica D. Petri Duzzinae de Anno 1575.

Cathedral Archives of Malta, Mdina

a. Archive of the Cathedral, Mdina:
    Ms. 454 Vol. I   Varia.

b. Archive of the Inquisition, Malta
    i. Criminal Proceedings:

Vol.	1A	1546-1578.
Vol.	2B	1563-1576.
Vol.	4A	1563-1578.
Vol.	6C	1581-1583.
Vol.	14A	1595-1598.
Vol.	14B	1595-1598.
Vol.	15A	1595-1598.
Vol.	15B	1595-1598.
Vol.	16A	1598-1600.
Vol.	17	1598-1600.

Vol.	18	1598-1600.
Vol.	19A	1600-1605.
Vol.	19B	1600-1605.
Vol.	20A	1600-1605.
Vol.	20B	1600-1605.
Vol.	22C	1600-1605.
Vol.	23A	1600-1605.
Vol.	23B	1600-1605.
Vol.	24A	1605-1607.
Vol.	26A	1605-1607.
Vol.	28B	1607-1608.
Vol.	28C	1607-1608.
Vol.	33A	1608-1614.
Vol.	33B	1608-1614.
Vol.	34B	1608-1614.
Vol.	38A	1615-1619.
Vol.	61A	1646-1649.
Vol.	146	1598.
Vol.	147A	1599-1600.
Vol.	147B	1599-1600.
Vol.	169	1601-1609.

ii. Civil Proceedings:
     Vol.   7   1597.

iii. Correspondence:
     Ms.   1   1588-1608.
     Ms.   2   1609-1612.
     Ms.   88   1577-1636.

iv. Miscellanea:
     Vol.   2   Pratica per procedere nelle cause del
                  sant'officio

Secondary Sources

Abela, G.F.: *Della Descrittione di Malta Isola nel Mare Siciliano, con le sue Antichità ed Altre Notitie,* Malta, 1647.

Anonymous: 'Relazione di Malta e suo inquisitoriato: dell'inquisitore Federico Borromeo', *Malta Letteraria,* vol. ii (1915), 47-56, 115-120, 149-153,185-191.

Baxter, C.: 'Johann Weyer's *De Praestigiis Daemonum:* Unsystematic psychpathology', Anglo, S. (ed), *The Damned Art. Essays in the Literature of Witchcraft,* London, 1977.

Benedeck, G.: 'The changing relationship between midwives and physicians during the Renaissance', *Bulletin of the History of Medicine,* vol. 51 (1977), 550-64.

Bonnici, A.: *Aspetti della Vita Cristiana nell'Isola di Malta Verso la Metà del Seicento,* Malta, 1974.

_____ :*Il-Maltin u l-Inkizizzjoni f'Nofs is-Seklu Sbatax,* Malta, 1977.

_____ :*Storja ta' l-Inkizizzjoni ta' Malta,* vols. I-III Malta, 1990 – 94.

Bonomo, G.: *Scongiuri del Popolo Siciliano,* Palermo, 1953.

_____ :*Caccia alle Streghe: La Credenza nelle Streghe dal Secolo XIII al Secolo XIX con Particolare Riferimento all'Italia,* Palermo, 1959.

Bossy, J.: *Christianity in the West: 1400-1700,* Oxford, 1985.

Braudel, F.: *The Mediterranean and the Mediterranean World in the Age of Philip II,* 2nd edn. 2 vols. Eng. trans. London, 1972-73.

Burke, P, 'Introduction: the development of Lucien Febvre', Burke, P. (ed), *A New Kind of History. From the Writings of Lucien Febvre,* London, 1973.

_____ : 'Witchcraft and magic in Renaissance Italy: Gianfrancesco Pico and his Strix', Anglo, S. (ed), *The Damned Art. Essays in the literature of witchcraft,* London, 1977.

_____ : *Popular Culture in Early Modern Europe,* London, 1978.

_____ : 'A question of acculturation?', *Scienze, Credenze Occulte, Livelli di Cultura: Convegno Internazionale di Studi,* Florence, 1982.

_____ : *The Historical Anthropology of Early Modern Italy,* Cambridge, 1987.

_____ : 'Popular piety', (J. O'Malley ed.) *Catholicism in Early Modern History. A Guide to Research,* St Louis, Missouri, 1988.

_____ : *Venice and Amsterdam. A study of Seventeenth-century Élites,* (2nd ed.) Cambridge, 1994.

Butler, E.M.: *Ritual Magic,* Cambridge, 1949.

Camenzuli, A.: 'Inquisition and Society in Mid-Eighteenth Century Malta', B.A. (Hons) unpublished dissertation, University of Malta, 1996.

Camporesi, P.: *The Incorruptible Flesh. Bodily Mutation and Mortification in Religion and Folklore*, Eng. trans. Cambridge,1988.

Cardozo, A.R.: 'A modern American witch-craze', Marwick, M.G. (ed), *Witchcraft and Sorcery,* Harmondsworth, 1982.

Cassar, C.: *'O Melita Infelix* – A poem on the great siege written in 1565', *Melita Historica*, vol. viii (1981), 149-155.

_____ : 'The first decades of the Inquisition: 1546-1581', *Hyphen – A Journal of Melitensia and the Humanities*, vol. iv (1985), 207-238.

_____ : 'The Reformation and sixteenth century Malta', *Melita Historica*, vol. x (1988), 51-68.

_____ : 'An index of the Inquisition: 1546-1575', *Hyphen – Journal of Melitensia and the Humanities*, vol. vi, (1990), 157-178.

_____ : 'Popular Perceptions and values in Hospitaller Malta', V. Mallia-Milanes (ed), *Hospitaller Malta 1530-1798: Studies on Early Modern Malta and the Order of St. John of Jerusalem*, 429-74, Malta, 1993.

_____ : 'Witchcraft beliefs and social control in seventeenth century Malta', *Journal of Mediterranean Studies*, vol.3, No.2 (1993), 316-34.

_____ : 'The Inquisition Index of Knights Hospitallers of the Order of St. John', *Melita Historica*, vol.xi (1993), 157-96.

_____ : 'Economy, society and identity in early modern Malta', unpubl. Ph.D. dissertation, University of Cambridge, 1994.

Cassar, P.: *Medical History of Malta,* London, 1964.

_____ : 'Healing by sorcery in seventeenth and eighteenth century Malta', *The St. Luke's Hospital Gazette*, vol.xi, No.2 (1976), 83-85.

Ciantar, G.A.: *Malta Illustrata, Ovvero, Descrizione di Malta Isola nel Mare Siciliano del Commendatore F. Giovan Francesco Abela Corretta, Accresciuta e Continovata dal Conte Giovannantonio Ciantar* Vol.II, Malta, 1780.

Ciappara, F.: 'Lay healers and sorcerers in Malta (1770-1798)', *Storja '78*, 60-76. Malta, 1978.

Cocchiara, G.: *Il Diavolo Nella Tradizione Popolare Italiana*, Palermo, 1945.

_____ : *Il Linguaggio della Poesia Popolare*, Palermo, 1951.

Cutajar, D. & Cassar, C.: 'Malta and the sixteenth century struggle for the Mediterranean', *Mid-Med Bank Report and Accounts*, 23-59, Malta, 1985.

Debono, J.: 'Heresy and the Inquisition in a Frontier Society, 1718-1720,' B.A. (Hons) unpublished dissertation, University of Malta, 1995.

De Giorgio, R.: 'Advice on the fortification of Mount Sceberras including Gerolamo Cassar's contribution to their improvement', *Proceedings of History Week 1983*, (1984), 73- 95.

Delumeau, J.: *Catholicism Between Luther to Voltaire: A New View of the Counter-Reformation*, Eng. trans. London, 1977.

de Martino, E.: *Sud e Magia*, Milan, 1966 ed.

De Rosa, G.: *Chiesa e Religione Popolare nel Mezzogiorno*. Bari, 1979.

Di Nola, A.: *Gli Aspetti Magico-religiosi di una Cultura Subalterna Italiana*, Turin, 1976.

Fenech, K.: *Idjomi Maltin,* (4th ed) Malta, 1970.

Febvre, L.: 'Witchcraft: nonsense or a mental revolution?', P.Burke (ed), *A New Kind of History. From the Writings of Lucien Febvre,* London, 1973.

_____ : *The Problem of Unbelief in the Sixteenth Century: The Religion of Rabelais,* Eng. trans. Cambridge Mass., 1982.

Flynn, M.: 'Blasphemy and the play of anger in sixteenth century Spain', *Past & Present,* 149 (1995), 29-56.

Forbes, T.R.: 'The regulation of English midwives in the sixteenth and seventeenth centuries', *Medical History,* (1964), 235-44.

Geertz, C.: *The interpretation of cultures,* London, 1993 ed.

Gentilcore, D.: *From Bishop to Witch: The System of the Sacred in Early Modern Terra d'Otranto,* Manchester, 1992.

Ginzburg, C.: 'Stregoneria, magia e superstizione in Europa fra medioevo ed età moderna', *Ricerche di storia sociale e religiosa,* vol. ix (1977), 119-33.

_____ : *The Cheese and the Worms: The Cosmos of a Sixteenth Century Miller,* Eng. trans. London, 1980.

_____ : *The Night Battles: Witchcraft and Agrarian Cults in the Sixteenth and Seventeenth Centuries,* Eng. trans. London, 1983.

_____ : 'The witches' sabbath: Popular cult or inquisitorial stereotype?', Kaplan, S. (ed.), *Understanding Popular Culture,* Berlin, 1984.

_____ : *Ecstasies. Deciphering the Witches' Sabbath,* Eng. trans. London, 1990.

Grendler, P.F.: *The Roman Inquisition and the Venetian Press: 1540-1605,* Princeton, 1977.

Gurevich, A.: *Medieval Popular Culture: Problems of Belief and Perception,* Eng. trans. Cambridge, 1988.

Henningsen, G.: '"Ladies from outside": an archaic pattern of the witches sabbath' Ankarloo, B. & Henningsen, G. (eds), *Early Modern European Witchcraft: Centres and Peripheries,* Oxford, 1989.

Horsley, R.: 'Who were the witches? The social roles of the accused in the European witch trials', *Journal of Interdisciplinary History,* vol.ix (1979), 689-715.

Kieckhefer, R.: *European Witch Trials: Their Foundations in Popular and Learned Culture, 1300-1500,* London, 1976.

_____ : *Magic in the Middle Ages,* Cambridge, 1989.

Larner, C.: 'Is all witchcraft really witchcraft?', *New Society,* vol.30 (1974).

_____ : 'Crimen exceptum? The crime of witchcraft in Europe', Gatrell, V.A.C. et al. (eds), *Crime and the Law: The Social History of Crime in Western Europe since 1500,* London, 1980.

Le Roy Ladurie, E.: *Montaillou. Cathars and Catholics in a French Village,* Eng. trans. Harmondsworth, 1980 ed.

Levack, B.P.: *The Witch-hunt in Early Modern Europe,* London, 1987.

Lewis, I.M.: *Ecstatic Religion: An Anthropological Study of Spirit Possession and Shamanism,* (2nd ed.) London, 1989.

Lopez, P. *Inquisizione, Stampa e Censura nel Regno di Napoli tra '500 e '600,* Naples, 1974.

Luttrell, A.T.: 'Approaches to Medieval Malta', Luttrell, A.T.(ed), *Medieval Malta. Studies on Malta Before the Knights,* London, 1975.

Macfarlane, A.: *Witchcraft in Tudor and Stuart England. A Regional and Comparative Study,* London, 1970.

Malinowski, B.: *Magic, Science and Religion and Other Essays,* London, 1974.

_____ : 'The role of magic and religion', Lessa, W.A. & Vogt, E.Z., *Reader in Comparative Religion – An Anthropological Approach,* New York, 1979.

Mallia-Milanes, V.: 'In search of Vittorio Cassar. A documentary approach', *Melita Historica,* vol.ix, (1986), 247-69.

Mangion, G.: 'Girolamo Cassar, architetto maltese del cinquecento', *Melita Historica,* vol. vii, (1973), 192-200.

Midelfort, H.C.E.: 'The social position of the witch in south western Germany', Marwick, M.G. (ed.), *Witchcraft and Sorcery,* Harmondworth, 1982.

Monter, W.: *Ritual, Myth and Magic in Early Modern Europe,* Brighton, 1983.

_____ : 'Women and the Italian Inquisitions', Rose, M. (ed), *Women in the Middle Ages and the Renaissance,* Syracuse N.Y., 1986.

Monter, W. & Tedeschi, J.: 'Toward a statistical profile of the Italian Inquisitions, sixteenth to eighteenth centuries', Henningsen, G. & Tedeschi, J. (eds.), *The Inquisition in Early Modern Europe: Studies on Sources and Methods,* Dekalb, 1986.

Murray, M.A.: *The Witch Cult in Western Europe,* Oxford, 1962 ed.

Nadel, S.F.: *Nupe Religion,* London, 1954.

Nauert, C.G.: _Agrippa and the Crisis of Renaissance Thought_, Urbana, 1965.

O'Neil, M.R.: ' _Sacerdote ovvero strione_'. Ecclesiastical and superstitious remedies in 16th century Italy', Kaplan, S.L. (ed), _Understanding Popular Culture. Europe from the Middle Ages to the Nineteenth Century_, New York, 1984.

_____ : 'Magical healing, love magic and the Inquisition in late sixteenth-century Modena', Haliczer, S. (ed), _Inquisition and Society in Early Modern Europe_, London, 1987.

Peters, E.: _Torture_, Oxford, 1985.

Pinto, L.B.: 'The folk practice of gynaecology and obstetrics in the Middle Ages', _Bulletin of the History of Medicine_, vol.47 (1973), 513-22.

Pitré, G.: _Fiabe, Novelle e Racconti del Popolo Siciliano_, vol. I. Palermo, 1875.

_____ : _Medicina Popolare Siciliana_, Palermo, 1894.

_____ : _Usi e Costumi, Credenze e Pregiudizi del Popolo Siciliano_, Vol.4, Florence 1949 ed.

Prosperi, A.: 'Intelletuali e chiesa all'inizio dell'età moderna', _Storia d'Italia. Annali IV: Intelletuali e potere_, Turin, 1981, 159-252.

Quaife, G.R.: _Godly Zeal and Furious Rage: The Witch in Early Modern Europe_, London, 1987.

Rivera, A.M.: _Il Mago, il Santo, la Morte, la Festa: Forme Religiose nella Cultura Popolare_, Bari,1988.

Romeo, G.: _Inquisitori, Esorcisti e Streghe nell'Italia, della Contro-riforma_, Florence, 1990.

Rowland, R.: '"Fantastical and devilish persons": European witch beliefs in comparative perspective', Ankarloo, B. & Henningsen, G. (eds.), _Early Modern European Witchcraft: Centres and Peripheries_, Oxford, 1989.

Salelles, S.: _De Materiis Tribunalium S. Inquisitionis: Seu Regulis Multiplicibus pro Formando Quovis Eorum Ministro, Praesertim Consultore, Praemissis xiii Prolegomenis de Origine et Progressu Dictorum Tribunalium_, Rome, 1651.

Sammut, E.: 'Girolamo Cassar, Architect of Valletta', _Annales de l'Ordre Souverain Militaire de Malte_', vol.xxiii, (1965), 22-34.

Savona-Ventura, C.: 'The influence of the Roman Catholic Church on midwifery practice in Malta', _Medical History_, vol.39 (1995), 18-34.

Schermerhorn, E.W.: _Malta of the Knights_, London, 1929.

Schmitt, J.C.: '"Religion populaire" et culture folklorique', _Annales ESC_, vol.31 (1976), 941-53.

Seppilli, T.: _Le Tradizioni Popolari in Italia: Medicina e Magia_, Milan, 1989.

Skorupski, J.: *Symbol and Theory: A Philosophical Study of Theories of Religion in Social Anthropology*, Cambridge, 1976.

Taylot, R.: 'Architecture and Magic', *Essays in the History of Architecture Presented to Rudolf Wittkower*, London, 1967.

Tedeschi, J.: 'The Roman Inquisition and witchcraft: An early seventeenth century "Instruction" on correct trial procedure', *Revue de l'Histoire des Religions*. CC (1983), 163-88.

_____ : 'Inquisitorial law and the witch', Ankarloo, B. & Henningsen, G. (eds), *Early Modern European Witchcraft: Centres and Peripheries*, Oxford, 1989.

Thomas, K.: *Religion and the Decline of Magic*, Harmondsworth, 1973.

Trevor-Roper, H.: *Religion, the Reformation and Social Change*, London, 1967.

Turner, V.: 'Social dramas and stories about them', *Critical inquiry*, vii (1980), 141-68.

Walker, D.P.: *Spiritual and Demonic Magic from Ficino to Campanella*, London, 1958.

Wettinger, G.: 'Some aspects of slavery in Malta, 1530-1800'. unpublished Ph.D. dissertation, University of London, 1971.

_____ : 'The gold hoard of 1525', *Melita Historica*, Vol.7 (1976), 25-33.

_____ : *The Jews of Malta in the Late Middle Ages*, Malta, 1985.

Yates, F.: *Giordano Bruno and the Hermetic Tradition*, London, 1964.

_____ : *The French Academies of the Sixteenth Century*, London, 1967.

_____ : *The Occult Philosophy in the Elizabethan Age*, London, 1979.

Index[1]

Self denouncements and other accusations before the Inquisition tribunal are marked by an asterisk (*) in the Index.

The Left within the Maltese Labour Movement
John Chircop

THE LEFT WITHIN THE MALTESE LABOUR MOVEMENT

John Chircop

The political scenario of the interwar years saw the rise of ardent leftist groups. Disturbing and provocative to the local *status quo* of the time, these men wrought their influence on the Maltese people. They were feared and closely monitored until the final clamp-down.

The Left within the Maltese Labour Movement gives a comprehensive account of the intellectual and political currents of the period. It is replete with extensive documentation, oral testimonies, secret dispatches, and numerous illustrations, many of which were never published before.

ISBN: 1-870579-10-0 (pbk)
Price: £16.95 / $25.00 (pbk)

Extent: 260pp; 215x140mm; (Illust. b/w)

Hospitaller Malta 1530-1798
Studies on Early Modern Malta and the Order of St John of Jerusalem
Edited by Victor Mallia-Milanes

This collection of 16 original research papers, seeks to understand Malta's position in its broader Mediterranean context, its gradual social and political transformation, its mental habits, aspects of its urban and economic development, its military and architectural reality, its varied artistic life, the effects of the Enlightenment on its Church-State relations, and the place it held in the complex politics of Revolutionary France. There is no doubt that behind the changes which early modern Malta experienced from 1530 to 1798 lay the powerful dynamism and resources of the Hospitaller institution of the Order of St John. Was not the nature of the island itself and its geographical location an equally powerful force which was partly to determine the direction of the Order's own development and decline? This volume is therefore as much concerned with early modern Malta as it is with the Order of St John.

ISBN: 1-870579-25-9 (pbk); 1-870579-15-1 (hbk)
Price: £19.95 / $35.00 (pbk); £40.00 / $70.00 (hbk)

Extent: 806pp; 215x140mm; (Illust. b/w)

Contents

A Note About These Stories

The stories of King Arthur are more than a thousand years old. They are stories; they are not history. But, history records the name of a war leader *Artorius* who lived around the year 500 AD. Perhaps the name 'Artorius' became 'Arthur' in the stories of King Arthur.

The Romans ruled Britain between 43 AD and 410 AD. Then, after the Romans left, there was no longer one government in the country. For centuries, there were many small kingdoms in Britain. The rulers of these kingdoms were warriors[1] or war leaders. These British leaders fought invaders[2] who came from the countries across the North Sea and the first stories of King Arthur date from about this time. But the most famous stories came from a later period.

The Roman Empire[3] became weak after the year 400 AD. During the next century, many different people moved across Europe from east to west. People from northern Germany and Scandinavia invaded Britain and drove the British people into the western and northern lands of Britain. These Anglo-Saxon invaders named the country Angleland, or England. Many years later, they became the English people and their language became English.

For two hundred years after this, Vikings from Scandinavia attacked[4] the coast of Britain. They also invaded France and mixed with Celts and Bretons. In France, the Vikings were called Normans – north men. Soon, these people no longer spoke German or Scandinavian. They spoke French and in 1066 AD, the Normans invaded Britain.

Over a century later, French poets and storytellers told the stories of King Arthur. They told the stories in the French language. Then, in the 14th century, poets and storytellers began to tell the stories in English. In these stories, a young man called Arthur became King of Britain. Arthur called the best warriors to his court[5] at Castle Camelot. The warriors, or knights, sat at a round table in the hall of the castle.

A magician[6] named Merlin helped Arthur to rule the land. These stories are about the Knights of the Round Table and their adventures. The stories describe how a good knight must behave. A good knight was chivalrous[7] and polite. He was a warrior and a powerful member of society. A knight supported his king and fought for honour, truth and justice[8]. He also went on quests[9]. He might have to kill an enemy or a dragon. Perhaps he had to save a young woman. Or he might have to find something that was holy or valuable. When he had done these things, his quest was completed.

Stories about Arthur have been retold many times. They are the subject of books, plays, films, operas and poems. In *The Lord of the Rings* and *The Hobbit* by J. R. R. Tolkien, Gandalf the Wizard is based on Merlin the Magician. In the *Star Wars* films, the Jedi Knights are based on the Knights of the Round Table.

A Picture Dictionary

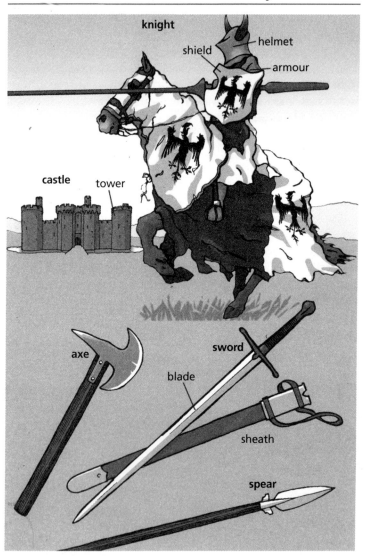

knight

shield

helmet

armour

castle

tower

axe

sword

blade

sheath

spear

The People in These Stories

Name	Role in the stories
Merlin the Magician	*a powerful wizard, guardian of Arthur*
Uther Pendragon	*King of Winchester*
Gorloïs	*King of Cornwall*
Igrayne	*Queen of Cornwall*
Morgana Le Fey	*a sorceress, half-sister of Arthur and mother of Mordred*
Arthur	*son of Uther Pendragon and Igrayne, King of Britain*
Ector	*an old knight, foster father of Arthur*
Kay	*son of Ector*
Bedivere	*the oldest knight of the Round Table*
Lancelot	*the bravest knight and Champion of Camelot, also lover of Queen Guinevere and father of Galahad*
Gawain	*the greatest knight*
Guinevere	*daughter of Leodogran and wife of Arthur*
Leodogran	*King of Cameliard*
Nimuë	*a sorceress and companion of Morgana*
The Green Knight	*Master of the Green Chapel*
Tristram	*Champion of King Mark of Cornwall, lover of Iseult the Fair*
Percivale	*the purest knight, afterwards guardian of the Grail Chapel*
Galahad	*the perfect knight, son of Lancelot, who achieves the Quest for the Holy Grail*
Meliot	*the wounded knight*
Gilbert	*the Black Knight*
Lady Gilbert	*a sorceress, also called Hellawes*
Elaine	*the Fair Maid of Astolat*
Iseult the Fair	*daughter of the King and Queen of Ireland, wife of King Mark and lover of Tristram*
Mark	*King of Cornwall*
Gurman	*King of Ireland*

7

The People in These Stories

Name	*Role in the stories*
Isaud	*Queen of Ireland*
Marhault	*Champion of Ireland*
Brangwain	*servant of Iseult the Fair*
Iseult of the White Hands	*wife of Tristram*
Kurwenal	*servant of Tristram*
Gareth	*a knight of Camelot*
Naciens	*the holy hermit of Carbonek*
Blanchefleur	*daughter of King Pelles and mother of Galahad, afterwards wife of Percivale*
King Pelles	*the wounded king, the old Grail Knight*
Bors	*a knight of Camelot*
Agravaine	*a knight of Camelot*
Mordred	*the evil knight, son of Arthur and Morgana Le Fey*
Lohengrin	*son of Percivale and Blanchefleur, also called Loherangrin or the Swan Knight*

1

The Coming of Arthur

Merlin the Magician and King Uther Pendragon

It was a time of war in Britain. There was much fighting and killing. There were many small kingdoms in Britain and each kingdom had its own king. But no king was strong enough to rule all the land. There was no peace in Britain and the people suffered.

Merlin the Magician spoke to the people. 'One king will come,' he said. 'All the land will become one kingdom. And one king will rule in one land. There will be peace at last.'

But who was this king? Perhaps it was Uther Pendragon, the King of Winchester. Uther was a strong king with a large army. He ruled most of southern Britain. Only the land of Cornwall, to the far west, had a king as powerful as Uther. The King of Cornwall was named Gorloïs.

King Uther spoke to Merlin the Magician. 'I will go to Cornwall,' said Uther. 'I will make peace with King Gorloïs. I will marry one of his daughters and we will have a son. Then our son will be King of all Britain.'

Merlin was silent. He looked at King Uther. Uther was short but he had a strong body. His hair and eyes were as black as the feathers of a raven[10]. Uther spoke loudly and roughly. Men were afraid of him because he was always angry. Uther rode a great warhorse and he carried a heavy sword. He could kill a man with one blow[11] of his sword.

Merlin was the opposite of Uther. Merlin was tall, but he was not strong. He did not carry a sword. Merlin's hair was as white as the feathers of a swan[12], but he was not an old man.

No one knew where Merlin came from. Some men said that Merlin came out of the west, from across the sea.

Merlin spoke quietly and said few words. But everyone listened to him when he spoke, because Merlin was wise and clever.

'Tell me, magician,' said Uther. 'Can you look into the future? Can you tell me – will my son be King of all Britain?'

Merlin was silent. His eyes were the colour of the clear blue sky. He did not look at the king; he looked far away. And there was sadness in Merlin's eyes when he spoke.

'Yes, Sire[13],' said the magician softly. 'Your son will be King of all Britain. But the unmarried daughter of King Gorloïs is very young. She is only a child.'

Uther Pendragon's face became bright with joy. 'Bring horses!' he shouted to his men. 'We will ride to Cornwall.'

Gorloïs – King of Cornwall

After many days, King Uther came to the land of Cornwall. He rode to Tintagel Castle, where King Gorloïs lived with his wife, Igrayne. The castle was built of black stone and stood on a high cliff above a dark sea.

'King Uther, you are welcome!' said Gorloïs. 'Eat and drink. We will be friends.'

So Uther and Gorloïs sat in the castle hall and ate and drank. King Gorloïs was an old, grey-haired man, but his wife, Igrayne, was young and very beautiful. Her hair was the colour of gold.

As soon as Uther saw Igrayne, he looked at no one else. He drank more and more wine and his face became red. He stared at Queen Igrayne. But she would not look at Uther. She lowered her eyes. King Gorloïs looked angrily at his guest.

10

'Tell me, lady,' said Uther to Igrayne. 'How many children do you have?'

'Three,' answered Queen Igrayne. 'My two older daughters are married. My youngest daughter is three years old. Her name is Morgana.'

Uther drank more wine. 'I can give you a son,' he said.

When King Gorloïs heard these words, he stood up and put his hand on his sword. 'Uther Pendragon! Leave my house now,' he shouted, 'and never return!'

Uther stood up slowly. 'I will leave,' he said to Gorloïs, 'but I will return with an army.'

And, so, King Uther made war against King Gorloïs. In October, Uther's army attacked Tintagel Castle. But Uther could not take the castle – it was too strong.

Igrayne – Queen of Cornwall

'I do not want Tintagel Castle,' Uther said to Merlin. 'I want Queen Igrayne. She will be my wife! Winter is coming and my men have little food. I will take the army back to Winchester. But first, I must have Igrayne. Help me, Merlin. And I will do anything that you say.'

'Tell your men to leave,' Merlin said. 'Tell them to move east, back towards Winchester. But tell them not to go far. They must wait in the woods. King Gorloïs will see that your men are leaving. He will come out of the castle and follow your army. Then you will go inside the castle and visit Igrayne.'

'The castle guards will kill me,' said Uther.

'I will protect[14] you,' said Merlin. 'I will use magic. I will cast a spell[15] and I will change you. For one night, I will give you the face and body of Gorloïs. But you must do one thing for me.'

'What do you want?' asked Uther Pendragon.

11

Uther Pendragon's promise to Merlin

'Igrayne will have a child,' said Merlin. 'You will give that child to me.'

'Yes,' said Uther. 'I will give you the child.'

So Uther gave orders to his men: 'Move away from the castle. Move back to the woods.'

The men walked away to the east, back towards Winchester. But they did not go far. Before night came, Uther's men stopped. They waited in the woods.

But Uther did not go with his men. He and Merlin hid in a circle of tall stones and waited. The king and the magician watched the gates of the castle. At last, the gates opened. King Gorloïs came out with his men and they followed Uther's army.

Merlin spoke words of magic. He cast a spell. Slowly, the shape of Uther's face and body changed until he looked like an old, grey-haired man. Uther had become Gorloïs!

Uther rode his horse to the gates of Tintagel Castle. 'Open the gates!' he ordered the guards. 'I will go to the Queen.'

Uther Pendragon went to the bedchamber of Queen Igrayne. And that night, there was a great storm. The wind blew from the sea and lightning lit the black walls of the castle. The sound of thunder was loud, but the sounds of battle were louder. The armies of Uther and Gorloïs were fighting with swords and axes. Igrayne cried out as she slept.

In the morning, Uther was gone. Igrayne went to the eastern walls of the castle and saw her husband's army returning. But King Uther's men were behind the army of Gorloïs and they were carrying her husband's body on a shield. King Gorloïs was dead. He had been killed in the battle and his body was covered in blood from many wounds[16].

Then Uther entered Tintagel Castle as himself and Igrayne became his wife.

The birth of Arthur

Uther stayed at Tintagel until the middle of the next year. On Midsummer's Day, Igrayne gave birth[17] to a son. But she did not give her son a name.

That night, Merlin came to the castle. Uther and Igrayne were holding their newborn son. Igrayne's daughter, Morgana, was with them.

Merlin did not speak to Uther and Igrayne. He took the baby boy and looked at him. 'I name you, Arthur,' he said.

'Give me my son!' Igrayne cried. But Uther remembered his promise and did not stop the magician. Merlin took the boy and went away.

Igrayne wept all night and all day. Slowly her sadness and pain made her go mad. She ran to the western walls of the castle and threw herself into the sea.

Morgana Le Fey and the death of Uther

Uther and his men left the castle. He took Igrayne's daughter, Morgana, with him. When he reached the town of Glastonbury he found a nunnery[18] with high walls. There, holy women – or nuns – lived and never went outside.

'Morgana will be a nun,' Uther said. 'She will stay inside the nunnery walls. No man shall see her face again.'

Then Uther returned to Winchester. He was now king in the south of Britain. There was peace in the land for a time, but Uther had many enemies.

One enemy, who lived in the north, sent a servant to work in the king's kitchen at Winchester. The servant put poison into King Uther's wine. Uther drank the wine and died at the table in the great hall of his castle.

13

Merlin promises a New King

For fifteen summers and winters, there was no king in the south and the people suffered because there was no order in the land. Then, one night, Merlin came secretly to Winchester. He went to Winchester Cathedral – the great church in the town – and spoke to the archbishop[19].

'Tell all the people to come to the cathedral on Sunday,' he said.

On Sunday, the knights and the people of Winchester came to the cathedral. They prayed for peace and a good king. And while they were praying, they heard a sound like music outside the cathedral.

The people went outside. In the field by the church, they saw a large stone. The stone was half as big as a man. A bright, metal sword was standing in the stone. The people could see only the handle of the sword.

The archbishop looked at the stone and the sword. Words were written on the stone in gold letters:

THE MAN WHO PULLS THIS SWORD FROM
THE STONE IS THE TRUE KING OF ALL
BRITAIN.

Then one by one, the men tried to pull the sword from the stone. All the knights of Winchester tried, but they all failed. The sword did not move.

'The true king is not here today,' said the archbishop. 'I will send messengers through all the lands of Britain. Soon, everyone will know about this sword. Anyone who wants to pull the sword out of the stone must come here at Christmas. On New Year's Day, we will have a contest. We will see who can draw the sword from the stone.'

The Sword in the Stone

The contest at Winchester

All the knights of Britain came to gather at Winchester. They put their tents in the fields near the cathedral. It was winter and very cold so the men lit fires to keep warm.

Sir Ector was an old, brave and honest knight. He came to Winchester with his two sons – Kay and Arthur. The three men rode their horses towards the cathedral. It was New Year's Day and they were going to the gathering of the knights.

Kay was eighteen years old and ready to become a knight. But only a king can give a man this title. And there was no king in the land.

Arthur was nearly sixteen years old. He did not look like his brother, Kay. Kay was dark-haired. But Arthur had fair hair, which was almost the colour of gold. Arthur was taller and stronger than his older brother.

Kay stopped his horse. Then he put his hand on his sheath and felt for his sword. But the sheath was empty. 'I have forgotten my sword,' he said to Arthur. 'I helped Father to put on his armour but I forgot to put my own sword in my sheath.'

'I will ride back to our tent,' said Arthur. 'The knights are gathering near the cathedral. Go there. I will fetch your sword and bring it to you.'

'Ride quickly,' said Kay.

So Arthur rode his horse back across the field. Then, in the middle of the field, he saw the stone and the sword. The bright sunshine shone on the sword.

'No one is using this sword,' Arthur thought. 'I will borrow it for my brother Kay.' Then the young man pulled the sword from the stone and took it to his brother.

Arthur takes the Sword

Arthur did not know why the sword was in the stone. But Kay knew about the sword and the other knights knew too. They all gathered around Kay and Arthur.

'Who gave you this sword?' asked a knight. 'What are you doing with it?'

'Arthur, this sword does not belong to you,' said Sir Ector. 'Put the sword back in the stone. The sword belongs to the true king.'

All the knights watched as Arthur put the sword back into the stone.

'Kay,' said Sir Ector. 'Draw the sword from the stone.'

So Kay put this hand around the handle of the sword and pulled. But the sword did not move. Then all the other knights tried to pull the sword out of the stone. Many strong men tried to take the sword, but it still did not move.

'Arthur,' said Sir Ector, 'draw the sword from the stone.'

Arthur put his hand on the sword and drew the sword from the stone easily. Then he raised the sword above his head and the metal flashed brightly in the sunlight. Everyone could see that Arthur held the sword.

Sir Ector got off his horse. He drew his own sword from its sheath and knelt down on the ground. He lowered his head and held the handle of his sword towards Arthur.

'Arthur,' said Ector. 'You are the true king of all the land and I am your servant.'

Arthur was astonished[20]. 'Father, put your sword away,' he said. He touched the hilt of Sir Ector's sword. Ector kissed the sword and put it back in its sheath.

'Arthur,' said Ector. 'You are the true king of
all the land and I am your servant.'

'Arthur, Sire. You must know the truth,' said Sir Ector. 'I am not your father. Merlin the Magician brought you to me more than fifteen summers ago when you were only a few days old. "Take this child into your home," Merlin told me. "The boy's name is Arthur. Take care of him. Arthur and Kay will be brothers."'

Arthur is crowned King

When they heard these words, everyone knelt down. Arthur was astonished and could not speak. Then the archbishop led Arthur to the cathedral. The archbishop took the sword and laid it on the altar. Then Arthur knelt in front of the altar and prayed.

For a day and a night, Arthur prayed in the great church. He asked God to help him. He wanted to be a good and just king.

Three months passed. At the beginning of spring, Arthur was crowned king in Winchester Cathedral. When the archbishop put the crown on Arthur's head, all the people shouted, 'LONG LIVE THE KING!'

Excalibur

A new sword

Merlin the Magician came to Arthur. 'Sire, you will fight many battles,' he said. 'You will need a new sword.'

'But I have a sword,' Arthur replied.

'The sword that came from the stone is not for fighting,' said Merlin. 'That sword is a sign[21] that you are king. It is the Sword of Right. Now you need a sword for battle. Your new sword will be the Sword of Might. It will be a powerful, fighting sword. You must not use this sword because you are angry. You must use it to do good. You must defend the weak against the strong. You must fight against evil and defend your land.

A journey to the west

Merlin took Arthur to the lands in the west. They travelled for many days. They went through great forests and passed the dark castle at Tintagel where Arthur was born. They rode onto high, bare hills and came near to the sea.

From the top of these hills, Arthur saw a valley and a lake. In the far west, past the lake, he saw a plain of sand. Beyond the plain of sand, he saw the sea. And, on the horizon, he could see a group of islands.

Arthur and Merlin rode down the hills and into the valley until they came to the edge of the lake. There, they stood together and looked at the water. Clouds moved across the sky and the colour of the water changed from blue to green to grey. As the sun went lower in the sky, a soft, white mist came across the water. And then a boat came out of the mist.

The boat was empty, and it had no sails or oars. There was no wind, but the boat moved slowly across the water until it stopped at Arthur's feet. Then Arthur stepped inside. The boat began to move towards the middle of the lake.

The Lady of the Lake

A hand and arm rose out of the water. The arm was covered in fine white cloth. The hand held a great sword. Arthur reached out and took the sword in his own hand. As he held the sword, a voice whispered the name, 'EXCALIBUR!' Then the arm disappeared under the water.

Arthur looked at the sword. It was made of fine steel and there was writing on the blade. The words, TAKE ME UP, were written on one side of the blade. On the other side of the blade, were the words: CAST ME AWAY.

The boat moved back to the shore where Merlin was waiting.

'The sword, Excalibur, is a gift from the Lady of the Lake,' Merlin said. 'One day, you must give it back to her.'

'How shall I know that day?' asked Arthur.

'You will know that day when you come to this lake again,' Merlin answered. 'Now, it is time for battle.'

Into battle

So Arthur returned to Winchester and gathered his knights.

'We shall go to the east and to the north,' he told them. 'We shall fight the invaders who attack the coast of our land. And we shall fight against the wild men of the north.'

Then Arthur led his men to the east and fought the invaders from the sea. The villagers in the east had left their homes and were hiding in the western lands. The villages were empty.

Arthur fought six battles. He carried the sword Excalibur into each battle and defeated his enemies. The invaders ran to their ships and went back across the sea.

When the invaders had gone, the people returned to their villages. At last there was peace in the southern and eastern lands.

Next, Arthur turned to the north. There he fought six battles against the wild men of the northern lands and won a great battle at Badon Hill. After this, there was peace in the northern lands too. The northern people made Arthur their king.

Arthur had been fighting for six long years.

The Kingdom of Logres

Arthur named all his lands the Kingdom of Logres. And, at last, there was one king ruling one country. It was a time of peace and plenty[22] and the people were happy.

Camelot and the Round Table

Arthur built a castle on a hill above a river. He named the castle Camelot. Castle Camelot was made of white stone and it had many towers.

The bravest knights of Logres came to Camelot and sat with Arthur in his great hall. In the centre of the hall there was a round table which had been made by Merlin.

Many knights sat and ate and drank at this round table. Camelot became the home of King Arthur and the Knights of the Round Table.

4

Queen Guinevere

The most famous Knights

Many knights joined King Arthur at Camelot. Three of those knights – Sir Bedivere, Sir Lancelot du Lac and Sir Gawain – would always be remembered.

Sir Bedivere was the first and most faithful knight. Sir Lancelot du Lac was the bravest, the strongest and the most handsome knight. And Sir Gawain was often called the Greatest Knight because Gawain was polite and chivalrous and he did great deeds[23].

As time passed, more knights came to Camelot. They, too, did many great and good deeds. All the knights sat in special seats at the Round Table. The seats were also called 'sieges'. Each knight's name was written on their siege in letters of gold. But one seat at the table was always empty. There was no name written on it.

The Siege Perilous

'The empty seat is called the Siege Perilous,' said Merlin. 'Only one man may sit in this place. The man will be pure – a man who has never done any evil deed. I do not know his name, but the man will come to Camelot one day. Meanwhile, no other man may sit on the Siege Perilous. If they do, they will die. Then great trouble will come to Logres.'

Leodogran – the King of Cameliard

The Knights of the Round Table travelled through all the land. There were no battles to fight now, but they fought other enemies – robbers, ogres[24], and evil magicians. Arthur's knights guarded and supported their king. They also protected the poor and weak.

During this time, Arthur rode west with Sir Gawain and Merlin until they came to the land of Cameliard. The King of Cameliard was called Leodogran.

Arthur, Merlin and Gawain stopped at King Leodogran's castle. Leodogran welcomed them and took them into his hall.

'You are welcome,' he said. 'Please eat, drink and rest in my castle.'.

King Leodogran was a tall man. He had a handsome and honest face and he smiled often. His daughter came into the hall and she smiled at the guests.

'This is my daughter, Guinevere,' said King Leodogran.

Guinevere was tall, and her face was very beautiful. Her hair was the colour of gold. Men said that she was the fairest and most lovely woman in the land. She came into the hall and sat on the left side of her father.

As soon as Arthur saw Guinevere, he looked at no one else. But Arthur did not behave like Uther Pendragon, his father. When Guinevere lowered her eyes, Arthur lowered his eyes too.

King Leodogran looked at them both and smiled.

Arthur spoke quietly to Merlin. 'I want to marry,' he said. 'The Kingdom of Logres must have both a king and a queen. And the kingdom must have an heir[25]. I must have a son who will be king after me. I choose Guinevere to be my Queen.'

Merlin looks into the future

Merlin looked at Arthur. The young king was tall and strong and his hair was the colour of gold. Arthur had a handsome face and clear eyes. When people looked at him, they thought of a lion. The king's voice was soft and when he spoke, men listened. Men loved Arthur because he was polite and honest and wise. They respected him because he was a great warrior and had won many battles. Arthur had brought peace to Logres.

'Merlin,' said Arthur. 'Can you look into the future? Use your magic and answer this question. Will my marriage to Guinevere bring peace and plenty to the Land of Logres?'

Merlin did not reply immediately. He looked far away towards the sea. His eyes were pale blue – the colour of the summer sky. Suddenly the colour of his eyes changed. They became dark grey – the colour of the sky during a storm.

There was sadness in Merlin's voice when he spoke. He said quietly: 'Yes, Arthur, the Land of Logres will know peace and plenty for a time. But all things must pass and all men must pass with them. Your kingdom will live in memory. Your story will last as long as men tell stories. But you shall pass away and I shall pass away and your kingdom shall pass away.'

'This is the way of the world,' said Arthur. 'I shall marry Guinevere and I shall love her and keep her. And I shall care for the land as long as I live.'

'Now I must tell you that I have looked into the future for the last time,' said Merlin. 'My powers are growing weak. My own future is dark, and, soon, I will pass away into the darkness. You will have to rule without my help. You are King Arthur and your queen shall be Guinevere. Rule the Land of Logres with justice. Make it a peaceful place.'

Arthur asks Guinevere to be his wife

Arthur went and spoke to King Leodogran. 'I wish to marry your daughter,' he said.

Leodogran looked at his daughter, Guinevere, and she smiled. 'I am happy,' said Leodogran. 'You are a great king. It will be a good marriage. And I see that my daughter is happy too.'

And so the kings made an agreement. 'I shall marry Guinevere in the spring,' Arthur said to Leodogran. 'Our wedding day will be on the holy festival which the English call Whitsun. And, before that day, I shall send my bravest knight to you. He will bring your daughter to Camelot. He will come to you in April, at the holy festival of Easter.'

'We shall wait for him at Caerleon Castle,' Leodogran said. 'Caerleon stands beside the River Usk. It is my favourite castle. I will give Caerleon Castle to you and to my daughter as a wedding gift.'

That night there was a great feast in the castle. Leodogran raised a cup and said: 'Let us drink to the health of King Arthur and Queen Guinevere.' And all the knights and people shouted: 'Long live King Arthur and Queen Guinevere!'

The Lady Nimuë

Arthur left Cameliard and rode with Merlin and Gawain to the south-west. Merlin led the way. At last, they came to a land of lakes.

'Why have we come this way?' asked Arthur.

'Someone is waiting for me here,' replied Merlin. 'I do not know who the person is, but, when I looked into the future, I saw this place.'

Nearby, they heard the sound of people fighting. Two knights were fighting beside the road. They fought with swords and shields. Two squires[26] held the knights' horses and watched the fight. A lady was standing between the two squires.

'Sirs! Why are you fighting?' Gawain called out to the knights.

'We are fighting for the lady,' one of the knights replied. 'You may not have her!'

As he said this, the knight lifted his sword and ran towards Gawain. Gawain raised his shield and drew his own sword from its sheath. The knight swung his sword and brought it down onto the neck of Gawain's warhorse, cutting off the horse's head. The horse dropped and Gawain was thrown to the ground.

'Knight!' shouted Gawain. 'Defend yourself!'

He jumped up, raised his own sword, and ran towards the knight. The knight lifted his shield, but Gawain was too strong. His sword broke the knight's shield. Then Gawain swung his sword at the knight's helmet and broke open his head. The knight fell down and died.

Then Gawain turned to the other knight, but the other did not wish to fight.

'I was defending the lady from this man, who is our enemy,' the other knight said. 'Her name is Lady Nimuë of Avalon. She is waiting for a messenger from King Arthur's court.'

Arthur and Merlin rode their horses forward. Gawain took the dead knight's horse.

'Who are you waiting for?' Arthur asked the lady.

Lady Nimuë smiled and said nothing. She looked at Merlin, and Merlin looked at Nimuë.

They said nothing, but Nimuë and Merlin spoke to each other without words. Nimuë was like Merlin. She had magical powers. She was a sorceress[27].

5

Merlin and Nimuë

Glastonbury and Morgana Le Fey

Arthur and Gawain rode along a narrow road across the watery land. Merlin followed them, carrying Nimuë on his horse. Merlin and Nimuë were always together. They used magic to speak together without words. Merlin was in love with Nimuë and he told her many secrets.

The group came to the town of Glastonbury which stands on an island in that watery land. A high hill rose behind the town and on that hill stood a small chapel. Next to it, there stood a nunnery with high walls.

Merlin and Nimuë climbed the hill. At the top they met a woman who was wearing the black clothes of a nun. Her head was covered so that no man could see her face. The woman seemed to be waiting for them.

'This lady is Morgana,' said Nimuë to Merlin. 'I have learnt magic from you. Now, Morgana will learn from you too.'

Merlin's magical powers were becoming weaker. He did not know it, but Nimuë was controlling the magician's mind. Merlin did not look at Morgana, because he only thought about Nimuë. He did not see that the nun was Morgana Le Fey – the daughter of Gorloïs and Igrayne of Cornwall. And Merlin did not remember that Morgana was Arthur's half-sister[28].

And so the two sorceresses – Nimuë and Morgana – learnt Merlin's secrets. They took more and more of the magician's power and Merlin gradually became old and weak.

The Holy Grail

Arthur and Gawain left the nunnery and went to Glastonbury Abbey[29]. Inside the abbey, there was a well of holy water. The abbess – the woman in charge of the nunnery – showed the holy well to Arthur and Gawain.

'Joseph of Arimathea[30] brought the Holy Grail to this land,' said the abbess. 'He put the Grail into this well. The water from this well can heal[31] the sick. The Grail itself can heal the land. It can stop troubles and bring peace. But the Grail was taken from us. It is not lost; it is hidden somewhere. Only the purest knight can find the Grail. He will find the Grail when there is great danger in the land.'

Merlin speaks to Arthur for the last time

Arthur, Gawain and Merlin rode back towards Camelot with Nimuë and Morgana Le Fey. Merlin spoke to Arthur.

'Sire, I shall not return to Camelot,' said the magician. 'I am going away with Nimuë and Morgana. You are king, and Guinevere is queen. You must rule without my help.'

Arthur was troubled by Merlin's words. 'Shall I never see you again?' Arthur asked.

'You will never see me in this life again,' answered Merlin. 'But we shall both return, one day. Remember, you are the Once and Future King. Now, goodbye. I shall see your wedding, and then I shall leave.'

Merlin's words made Arthur sad. But as he rode on to Camelot with Gawain, he did not think deeply about their meaning.

Lancelot becomes Champion of Camelot

Shortly before the holy week of Easter, Arthur sent for Sir Lancelot. Sir Lancelot was the strongest and most handsome

the Knights of the Round Table. He always wore shining armour.

'Lancelot,' Arthur said. 'You are my bravest knight. I now make you my Champion Knight. You will guard and defend everything that I love. Ride to Caerleon Castle. My bride, Guinevere of Cameliard, is waiting there. Bring Guinevere to Camelot. She and I will be married at Whitsun. Then Guinevere will be crowned Queen.'

Lancelot smiled and bowed towards the king. 'Yes, Sire,' he said. Then he got onto his great warhorse, which was dressed in red and white cloth, and he rode away.

Lancelot meets Guinevere

Lancelot's journey to Caerleon took many days. At last he came to the castle where Guinevere was waiting.

When he met Guinevere, he saw that she was the fairest woman in the land. And Guinevere saw that Lancelot was the fairest man.

Lancelot and Guinevere rode to Camelot together, talking and laughing. Behind them rode twenty of Leodogran's finest knights. Each knight wore fine armour and fine clothes.

It was the month of May and white flowers fell from the trees onto the road. The travellers stopped and rested at a chapel where many flowers grew. Lancelot took a red rose and put it in his hair. Guinevere took a white lily and wore it on her dress.

'Lady,' said Lancelot. 'I am your servant. I shall always serve you and no other.'

The marriage of Arthur and Guinevere

They came to Camelot and saw that there were many tents in the fields. Knights had come to Camelot from many parts of Logres. Each day, the knights competed in jousts[32]. They rode their warhorses and fought with swords, shields and spears. And each evening, the knights ate, drank and told stories.

At Whitsun, Arthur married Guinevere. When he placed a crown upon her head, the knights and people gave a great cry. 'Long Live King Arthur and Queen Guinevere!' they shouted.

Morgana Le Fey plots the destruction of Camelot

That night, Merlin lay in his tent. With him were Nimuë and Morgana.

Merlin's mind was clouded and his sight was weak. He saw Morgana's smile but he did not see *behind* the smile.

Morgana hated her half-brother, Arthur, because his father, Uther Pendragon, had put Morgana in a nunnery. Because Merlin had taken Arthur away from Igrayne, Igrayne had thrown herself into the sea. Morgana hated Merlin as well.

While Merlin slept, Morgana cast two spells. The first spell was for Guinevere. It made Guinevere sleep in her own bedchamber and dream of Lancelot. With the second spell, she made herself look like Guinevere. Then she went to Arthur's bedchamber where Arthur was sleeping. He was dreaming of battle and wounds. He dreamt that he lost his sword, Excalibur. He dreamt that nothing grew on the land. Then Morgana came to Arthur's bed and lay with him.

As the sorceress lay with the king, bright lightning flashed in the sky. And when Morgana left Arthur, she whispered to her half-brother. 'I will have a son,' she said. 'He will be like your father, Uther Pendragon. Sleep well, brother.' And Arthur slept and forgot his dreams.

And so Morgana brought evil and sadness to the court of Camelot. Though, many long years passed before anyone knew that this had happened.

The passing of Merlin

Early the next morning, Merlin left his tent. He had become an old man. He was so ill and weak that Nimuë and Morgana had to help him onto his horse. Then they led the magician away from Camelot, towards the north.

'Merlin, I know a place where you will be young again,' said Nimuë. 'It is a secret place in a forest. We will take you there and you can rest.'

'Yes, yes,' said Merlin. But he did not see who spoke to him, or what was near him. He did not see the trees of the great forest around him. He did not see how they had come to a secret place in the forest where a circle of tall stones stood around a low hill. On the top of the hill, there was a great oak tree. Nimuë and Morgana led Merlin to the tree. Then, a doorway opened in the trunk of the tree. A light was burning inside.

'Step inside the tree, Merlin,' said Nimuë. 'Here you will find rest. You are old and tired. Soon you will feel young again. Here you may sleep through many centuries and dream of the world outside. Rest here – until the day when you shall wake and return to the land again.'

Merlin stepped into the oak tree and the door closed behind him. There, inside the oak, he slept and dreamed of the world outside.

'No man shall see his face again,' said Morgana to Nimuë.

From that day, no one saw Merlin the Magician again. But the people often spoke his name and told their children stories about him.

31

6

Sir Gawain and the Green Knight

Christmas court

It was a time of peace in the Kingdom of Logres. King Arthur and Queen Guinevere ruled wisely and well. Many good and noble[33] knights visited Camelot and the Round Table. Many stories were told of famous knights there – of Lancelot, Gawain, Tristram, Percivale and Galahad. And their stories are still told today.

Every year, on Christmas Day, King Arthur gathered the knights at his court in Camelot. Everyone celebrated for twelve days. There was a great feast. Everyone ate good food and drank wine. They danced and listened to stories.

Then, one year, on the twelfth day of Christmas, a strange knight rode into the court. He was the strangest knight that anyone had seen. He was tall and broad, like the trunk of a tree. His great warhorse had fierce, red eyes. The knight was not wearing armour, but he and his horse were both dressed in green cloth.

Even more strangely, both the knight and his horse were green. The skin of the horse was green and the skin of the knight was green. The knight's hair and beard were green too. The Green Knight did not carry a sword. He held a huge green and gold axe in his right hand.

The knight rode his horse through the gates of Camelot Castle. He rode into the great hall and stopped in front of the Round Table. Here, the best knights sat in the most important seats. Only one seat still remained empty at the table. This was the Siege Perilous.

The Green Knight looked around the hall. 'Where is the

king of this land?' he asked in a loud voice. 'I will speak with the king and no other man.'

The guests at the feast were astonished. No one had ever seen such a knight. He was the colour of new grass and leaves in spring. And he had ridden his horse into the hall!

'Sir knight, you are welcome,' said Arthur. 'Will you join us at the feast?'

'I do not come to eat and drink,' said the Green Knight. 'I come to see the brave and famous knights at your court.'

'Sir, there are many good knights here,' said Arthur. 'And many of them are ready to fight and to joust.'

The Green Knight challenges[34] the knights of Camelot

'I come from my castle in the north,' said the Green Knight. 'I make this challenge. Who will strike me with my own axe? Is any knight brave enough?'

He held the heavy green axe above his head. The knights of Camelot looked at it and were silent.

'Come, any man,' said the Green Knight. 'Take my axe. You may strike the first blow. You may cut off my head. I will strike the second blow. That is my only request.'

No one spoke. The Green Knight laughed. 'Are there no brave knights here? Do you all fear me? I speak truthfully. You may strike the first blow and I shall strike the second.'

'If no man will take your challenge,' said Arthur, 'I shall strike the blow myself. But you do not bring honour to my court. Your challenge is not honourable. Go in peace and do not return. This is a feast day, not a day of battle.'

Sir Gawain takes the challenge

The Green Knight laughed again. 'You fear that you cannot kill me with one blow from my axe,' he shouted. 'You fear that I will kill you. Is this what you brave men of Camelot think?'

'Who will strike me with my own axe?'

Then Gawain stood up. 'I am Gawain, son of King Lot,' he said. 'I will strike you with your axe. I will cut off your head.'

'Do it,' said the Green Knight. 'Then, after this day, twelve months and one day will pass. At that time, you shall come to my castle in the north. There I shall strike you with my axe and I will cut off your head. This will be our bargain[35].'

'Give me the axe,' said Gawain. 'I accept your bargain. But I will strike only once and you will never strike your own stroke. Go in peace, or you will die today.'

The Green Knight laughed. He got down from his horse and gave his axe to Gawain. Then he knelt down on the floor. 'Strike my neck, knight,' he said. 'Strike well. Remember our bargain.'

Sir Gawain took the green axe. It was a heavy axe and Gawain held it in both hands. 'I am a Knight of the Round Table,' he said. 'I do not break my word; but I give you a last chance to change your mind and leave in peace.'

'Strike!' shouted the Green Knight. 'What are you waiting for? Are you afraid? Strike me with my axe and cut off my head.'

Gawain raised the axe in both hands and struck the Green Knight's neck. The Green Knight's head rolled onto the floor.

The Green Knight is not dead

Then the knights and ladies of Camelot watched with astonishment. The Green Knight stood up. Then he picked up his head and held it by the hair. The eyes in the head looked at Gawain and the mouth moved and it spoke these words: 'I am the Knight of the Green Chapel in the north. You will come to the Green Chapel in one year and one day. Then I will cut off your head.'

Then, holding his head in his hand, the Green Knight got onto his horse. He rode out of the hall and out of Castle Camelot.

Everyone was silent. The feast was ended. 'Gawain has made a terrible bargain,' thought the Knights of the Round Table. 'He has just agreed to his own death.'

Sir Gawain journeys north

The year passed quickly. On the first day of the twelfth month, Arthur and his courtiers were at Caerleon. The knights said goodbye to Gawain.

Gawain put on his armour and his sword. He got onto his warhorse. A squire gave Gawain his shield. 'I will begin my quest,' said Gawain. 'I will go and look for the Green Chapel. I do this for the honour of Camelot and the glory of Logres.'

Gawain's journey was long and dangerous. He rode north into the forests where dark creatures lived. He did battle with robbers and ogres. He crossed rocky hills of stone and snow and cold streams where the ice broke. It was deep midwinter and colder than any man could remember. He stopped at every village and asked where he could find the Green Chapel.

At last, Gawain came to a deep valley. A wide stream ran in the bottom of this valley. On the other side of the stream, there was no snow on the ground. Here, the grass was green.

On the other side of the valley, there was a castle on a hill. Gawain went into the valley and rode through the stream. Then he went up to the castle and knocked on the gate.

'I am Gawain, from the court of King Arthur!' he shouted. 'I am seeking the Green Chapel.'

A servant opened the castle gate. 'My lord says that you are welcome,' said the man. 'Please come into the castle and rest.'

Gawain went into the castle. The servant took his horse to the stables. Then he led Gawain into the castle hall.

The lord of the castle was a tall man who had a thin, pale face. 'Welcome, Sir Gawain,' said the lord. 'It is Christmas – a time of peace and celebration. Will you stay with us and rest?'

Gawain sat by the warm fire. 'I thank you, sir,' he said. Then he ate the good food that the lord of the castle gave him.

'I seek the Green Chapel and the Green Knight,' said Gawain, when he had finished eating.

'The Green Chapel is near here,' replied the lord. 'You will find it at the end of this valley. But the Green Knight is a cruel man. Do not seek him. He will kill you.'

'I have made a bargain with the Green Knight,' replied Gawain. 'And I must keep this promise. I am a Knight of the Round Table. I cannot break my promise.'

'Very well,' said the lord of the castle. 'Rest here and you will find the Green Chapel tomorrow.'

The lady of the castle gives Gawain a green ribbon

The lady of the castle took Gawain to a bedchamber. The room was warm and the bed was soft. The lady brought hot wine to Gawain and smiled. She spoke softly and laughed easily. Gawain saw that she was very beautiful.

'You are a handsome knight,' said the lady. 'It is a cold night. Would you like a maiden[36] of the castle to visit you?'

'No, lady,' said Gawain. 'I thank you for the food and the fire. But I am on a quest. I will not bring honour to you or your lord if I spend time with your maidens.'

'You are a good and honorable knight,' said the lady. 'I have a gift for you. It is a small thing – a piece of green ribbon[37]. The ribbon will protect you. You must wear it in your hair.'

So Gawain tied the green ribbon in his hair. Then he slept.

The Green Chapel

Early the next morning, Gawain rode out of the castle and rode along the valley until he saw the Green Chapel. Outside the chapel sat the Green Knight. His head was back on his shoulders and his green face was angry.

The Green Knight was sharpening the blade of his axe.

'You have come a long way, Sir Gawain,' said the Green Knight. 'I am surprised. You have made a long journey to die.'

'I am here because I made you a promise,' answered Sir Gawain. 'I am a Knight of the Round Table at Camelot and I do not break my promises.'

'Very well,' said the Green Knight. 'Then you must prepare to die.'

Sir Gawain watched and waited as the Green Knight came close and swung his axe. Gawain heard the sound of the blade as it went through the air. But Gawain's head did not fall from his neck. Something else fell to the ground. It was the green ribbon – the gift from the lady of the castle.

Sir Gawain keeps his promise

Suddenly the face of the Green Knight changed. His skin was no longer green. His hair and beard were no longer green. Instead he became a tall man with a pale, thin face. He was the lord of the castle where Gawain had rested. Then his lady came out of the Green Chapel and stood beside her lord. She smiled at Gawain.

'The green ribbon was a sign to my husband,' she said. 'It is a sign that you are a man of honour.'

'Sir Gawain, you have proved that you are a good and honorable knight,' said the lord of the castle. 'Now you must return to Camelot and tell this story. From this day forward, men will say: "Sir Gawain did not break his promise to the Green Knight."'

7

The Chapel Perilous

Sir Lancelot seeks adventure

Sir Lancelot du Lac rode out of Camelot in search of adventure. He rode for many days until he found a forest full of tall trees that hid the sun. There were many paths through the trees, but Lancelot did not know which one to take.

Suddenly a white hunting dog came out of the trees. The dog put its nose to the ground and ran along one of the paths.

'Perhaps the dog will lead me to its master,' thought Lancelot. So Lancelot followed the dog along the path.

Lancelot looked at the ground and saw that there was a trail of blood on the path. The dog was following the trail of blood and Lancelot followed the dog. The dog kept turning its head to look at Lancelot.

The dog led Lancelot out of the forest. They went over a bridge to a large house. When the dog ran into the house, Lancelot got off his horse. He went into the house and saw a knight lying on the floor of the hall. The knight was wearing black armour. Blood ran from many wounds on the knight's body. He was dead.

Lancelot heard a sound outside the house. He went outside and saw a lady in the garden. Her hands were covering her eyes and she was crying.

The curse of Lady Gilbert

'What has happened?' Lancelot asked. The lady took her hands from her face and raised her head. Lancelot saw that she had an ugly red mark on her face.

'Sir Meliot came here,' answered the lady. 'He fought my husband and killed him. But Sir Meliot was wounded in the fight. The wound will never heal and Sir Meliot will die.'

'I know Sir Meliot,' said Lancelot. 'He is a Knight of the Round Table at Camelot. He is a good and honorable knight.'

The lady looked angrily at Lancelot. 'Go back to Camelot!' she cried. 'I am Lady Gilbert. My husband, Sir Gilbert, is the dead knight. I can make magic. I have cursed Sir Meliot. Now his wound will never heal. Go! ... or I will curse you too!'

Lancelot quickly left the house. The white hunting dog was waiting for him outside. The dog barked and ran along a path. Lancelot got onto his horse and followed. He rode back into the dark forest.

Soon they came to another large house. Another lady was sitting in the garden. She too, was crying, but as soon as she saw Lancelot she dried her eyes. The dog went to the lady and licked her hand.

Sir Meliot has a wound that will not heal

'I know you,' said the lady, 'You are Sir Lancelot du Lac. You know my brother, Sir Meliot.'

'Did Sir Meliot fight with Sir Gilbert today?' asked Lancelot.

'Yes, he did,' answered Sir Meliot's sister. 'Lady Gilbert is an evil sorceress. She has used magic. She has put a curse on Sir Meliot. He is wounded and his wound will not heal.'

Lancelot went into the house and found Sir Meliot lying in the hall. The knight had a bleeding wound on the left side of his body.

'Only a cloth from Chapel Perilous will heal my brother,' said Sir Meliot's sister. 'That is what Lady Gilbert told me.'

'Then I will go to Chapel Perilous and find this cloth,' said Lancelot.

'No man has gone into Chapel Perilous and returned alive,' said the lady. 'The chapel is in the middle of the forest. The knights who guard it are really dead but they still seem alive. They are controlled by Lady Gilbert's magic powers.'

'I do not fear any knights – living or dead,' said Lancelot.

'Then follow this path,' said the lady. She pointed to a path through the forest. 'The path is too narrow for your horse. You must walk. But Chapel Perilous is not far. Take my dog. The dog will guide you.'

Lancelot walked along the path until he came to the middle of the forest. Here, he saw a small chapel that was made of dark stones. The shields of many knights were hanging on a tree outside the chapel. These shields were upside down, which was a sign that the knights were dead.

The dead knights

The knights were standing near their shields. They did not move. Their armour was old and dark and they held swords in their hands. Lancelot stepped closer to them.

The knights turned slowly and looked at Lancelot. He saw their faces and knew that the knights were dead men. These were the knights who had entered Chapel Perilous. The knights opened their mouths but they could not speak. They looked at Lancelot with empty eyes.

Lancelot drew his sword and ran towards the knights. He swung his sword, but it passed straight through the bodies of the knights. And the knights could not strike Lancelot with their swords. The knights who guarded the chapel were ghosts.

Sir Lancelot enters the Chapel Perilous

So Sir Lancelot entered the Chapel Perilous. There were no windows in the walls, but many lamps hung from the ceiling.

Strange shadows moved on the walls. At the end of the chapel, there was a large, flat stone. The body of a knight was lying on this stone. Lancelot went to the body and saw that it was covered with a silk cloth. He cut a piece of the cloth with his sword and held it in his hand.

Suddenly, there was a sound like thunder. Then the floor moved. Lancelot walked back to the doorway and went outside. The dead knights stood in front of Lancelot and he could not pass. The ghosts did not move their mouths, but Lancelot heard their terrible voices.

'Knight! Do not take the cloth from the chapel,' they said. 'If you take the cloth, you will die. And you will never see Guinevere again.'

'Ghosts! You have no power over me,' said Lancelot. 'Let me pass.'

Lancelot swung his sword at the dead knights. But he could not fight them. The knights did not have bodies like living men. Instead, they pushed against Sir Lancelot like the thick smoke of a fire.

Lancelot swung his sword, but he could not fight smoke. Then, looking up into the light, Lancelot saw the shields that hung on chains above the entrance to the chapel. Lancelot cut at the chains and the shields began to fall. As one by one, each shield fell, one by one, a dead knight fell to the ground. When Lancelot had cut down all the shields, all the knights had fallen. Then Lancelot heard a great cry. The Lady Gilbert was standing at the entrance to the Chapel Perilous. She put her hand to the red mark on her face and then she too sank to the ground.

Sir Lancelot takes the cloth to Sir Meliot

Lancelot walked back to the house of Sir Meliot. The sun was bright and birds sang. Lancelot gave the cloth from Chapel

Perilous to Sir Meliot's sister. She smiled. 'Thank you,' she said. Then she led Lancelot to her brother.

'The Lady Gilbert is dead,' said Sir Lancelot. 'I have brought a cloth from the Chapel Perilous to heal your wound.'

Sir Meliot's skin was pale and he was near to death. Blood flowed from the wound in his side but as soon as the cloth touched his wound, the blood stopped flowing. Then Sir Meliot opened his eyes.

'I am healed,' he said. 'Lady Gilbert was an evil sorceress whose real name was Hellawes. She was a companion[38] of Morgana Le Fey. The power of Hellawes is broken now. But she cast a spell on another lady who lives near this forest. And that spell may not be broken.'

'I will return to Camelot,' said Lancelot. 'And I will tell the story of Hellawes the Sorceress and Chapel Perilous.'

Sir Meliot and his sister thanked Lancelot.

'Farewell,' said Lancelot. 'Sir Meliot, we will meet again, at the Round Table in Camelot.'

The Fair Maid of Astolat

Lancelot rode through forests until he came to a river that runs down to Camelot. A tall grey tower stood on an island in the river. The island was called the Isle of Astolat. Elaine, the Fair Maid of Astolat, lived in the tall tower.

No man had seen Elaine. She lived in the highest room of the tower. The room's walls had no windows, but it was bright because light came through windows in the ceiling. There were many mirrors on the walls that reflected this light. Elaine looked at the mirrors and she saw the world outside her tower.

The tower of mirrors

Years before, when the sorceress Hellawes gained her evil powers, her face had been spoilt with an ugly red mark. After that, Hellawes hated all beautiful women.

'No man wishes to see my face,' she said. 'But all men wish to see the face of the Fair Maid of Astolat. So I will put a curse on her. If Elaine looks at any man, she will die.'

Elaine knew that she could not look at the world outside her tower. And, so, she watched the world with her mirrors and she used coloured silk threads to make a tapestry[39]. The tapestry showed pictures of the world.

When Sir Lancelot came riding out of the forest, the sunlight flashed on the knight's bright armour. Elaine saw the bright flash in her mirror. She watched the knight as he rode closer to her tower. Lancelot was not wearing a helmet, so Elaine saw his face clearly.

Elaine had seen men reflected in her mirror, but she had never met a man. And she had never seen a man as handsome as Lancelot. She did not want the reflection of Lancelot to disappear from her mirror.

Forgetting the curse, Elaine ran from her room to the top of the tower. She opened the door and looked down at the knight's handsome face. But Lancelot did not see Elaine.

The curse

Suddenly the room at the top of the tower became dark. Sunlight no longer shone onto the mirrors and at once there was a great noise. The mirrors had broken and the floor was covered with broken glass.

Elaine fell to the floor. 'The curse has come to Astolat!' she cried.

Then she slowly walked down the stairs of her tower and went outside into the sunlight for the first and last time in her life. She walked to the river.

Sir Lancelot rode on towards Camelot. He heard and saw none of these things on the Isle of Astolat. He thought only of Camelot. Castle Camelot was near and he wanted to see Guinevere again. He thought of telling stories at the Round Table.

The death of Elaine

That day, there was a feast in Camelot. All the courtiers, knights and ladies ate and drank in the great hall. King Arthur and Queen Guinevere listened to stories of Sir Lancelot's adventures. But, in the middle of the feast, there was a sudden storm outside. The knights, ladies and courtiers went silent and the musicians stopped playing their music. And in the silence, they heard someone singing a sad song. The music came from outside the castle, from the direction of the river.

Everyone went to the windows and looked out from the towers of Camelot. They saw a boat floating along the river. In the boat sat a fair maiden who was singing the sad song. Before the boat reached Camelot, the maiden lay down and died.

All the people left the castle and went down to the river. The boat was dressed with brightly-coloured cloth and the maiden lay on soft, silk cushions. Her body was covered with a long tapestry with pictures made from coloured silk threads. The words, THE MAID OF ASTOLAT, were written on the boat.

Lancelot looked at the dead maiden. 'She has a beautiful face,' he said.

8

Tristram and Iseult

A minstrel[40] comes to Camelot

King Arthur sat at the Round Table and Lancelot and Gawain sat opposite him. But the seat between Lancelot and Gawain, the Siege Perilous, was still empty.

'No man has ever sat in the Siege Perilous,' said Arthur. 'Merlin told us many years ago that only the purest knight would sit in this place. But who will that knight be?'

'Perhaps it will be a knight who has not yet come to Camelot,' said Gawain.

'Sire,' said Lancelot. 'A minstrel has come to Camelot who plays a harp[41] and tells stories. He has travelled to Ireland and knows many stories. Perhaps he can tell us the name of a famous knight whom we do not know.'

So Arthur called the minstrel to the great hall. All the knights and their ladies sat and waited for the minstrel to tell a story.

The minstrel was tall and he had a fair face. But his clothes were poor and his shoes were old. He held a harp in his hand. He touched the strings of the harp with his fingers and it made a sweet sound.

The story of Tristram

'I will tell the story of Tristram,' the minstrel said in a clear voice. 'Tristram is a knight of Lyonesse – a land in the far west. King Mark of Cornwall is Sir Tristram's uncle.

'Before Arthur became king, there was war between Cornwall and Ireland. The rulers of Ireland were King Gurman and Queen Isaud. The armies of Cornwall and Ireland fought each other and Cornwall was defeated.

'Isaud's brother, Marhault, was a fierce warrior. He was the King of Ireland's champion. Marhault had black hair, cruel eyes and strong hands. He left Ireland and went to Cornwall. He spoke to King Mark.

'"The people and the land of Cornwall belong to King Gurman of Ireland now," said Marhault. "You must send a gift to Ireland. You must send fifteen boys and fifteen girls to be servants in Ireland."'

The gift

'But King Mark replied: "No! I will not send this gift."

'"Then tell your champion to fight me," said Marhault to Mark. "I am the Champion of King Gurman of Ireland and I can kill any man here. You must either fight me or send the gift to Ireland."

'At first no knight stepped forward to fight Marhault. But then a young man named Tristram stood up. "I will fight Marhault and bring honour to my king," he said.

'So Marhault laughed and drew his sword. "It will take only a moment to kill this boy," he said.

'Tristram drew his sword too. The two men fought a long and hard fight. After a time, Marhault struck a terrible blow to Tristram's leg. Then Tristram struck a blow to Marhault's head. Both men were badly wounded.

'Marhault fell to the ground. "My sword is poisoned!" he shouted to Tristram. "Your wound will not heal. You will die."'

The minstrel was silent for a moment. Everyone in the hall of Camelot was enjoying this story.

'Please continue,' said King Arthur.

The minstrel bowed to the king and continued his story.

Tristram's wound

'So Marhault's men carried their master to his ship and they sailed to Ireland. Marhault's sister, Queen Isaud, was a skilful healer. But Marhault's wounds were very bad and even Queen Isaud could not save him. And soon he died.

'Meanwhile, Tristram lay in the castle at Tintagel. No one could heal his wound.

'"Queen Isaud of Ireland is the most powerful healer in the world," said the wise men of King Mark's court. "Only Queen Isaud can heal this young man's wound. But Isaud is the enemy of Cornwall."'

When they heard this, some of the ladies of King Arthur's court began to cry.

The minstrel held up his hand. 'My story has not ended,' he said.

King Gurman and Queen Isaud

'Tristram went to Ireland. He could not walk because of the wound on his leg. Two servants carried him to the court of King Gurman. Tristram wore the clothes of a minstrel and he sang songs. Tristram sang so well that King Gurman asked him to sing in the hall of his castle.

'"How did you receive your wound?" asked King Gurman.

'"I was travelling on a ship to Ireland," Tristram replied. "Pirates[42] attacked the ship and I was wounded. The pirates killed all the other men on the ship, but they did not kill me. The pirates let me live because I played the harp and sang so well."

'Queen Isaud believed Tristram's story. "I will heal your wound," she said. And she took the minstrel to a room where he stayed for many days. Queen Isaud cared for him and healed his wound.

'After he became well, Tristram stayed in Ireland. He played the harp and sang at the court.'

Iseult the Fair

'Gurman and Isaud had one child – a daughter. The girl's name was Iseult and all men called her Iseult the Fair.

'King Gurman asked Tristram to teach his daughter. "I want Iseult to sing and to play the harp," said the king. "Please be her teacher."

'So Tristram stayed in Ireland and taught Iseult. Tristram quickly began to love Iseult, but he told no one of his feelings.

'After a time, Tristram left Ireland and returned to Cornwall. He told King Mark what had happened in the court of King Gurman and Queen Isaud. Then a wise man spoke to King Mark.

'"Sire, there is a way to end the war between Cornwall and Ireland," he said. "If you marry Iseult the Fair, there will be peace."

'King Mark thought carefully. "I have heard of Iseult the Fair," he said. "All men speak of her beauty. I will marry her and bring peace to Cornwall and Ireland. But will Gurman and Isaud agree?"'

The minstrel paused a moment. His face was sad. Then he continued his story.

The Dragon[43] of Ireland

'At that time, there was a dragon that lived in Ireland. This huge, terrible creature breathed fire from its mouth. It used that fire to destroy many villages. It killed hundreds of men, women and children.

'"Whoever kills the dragon can marry my daughter," King Gurman told his knights. "And he shall have half of my kingdom as a wedding gift."

'Tristram heard King Gurman's promise. He put on his sword and his armour, and he returned to Ireland. He did not go to the court of King Gurman and Queen Isaud. He went straight to the place where the dragon lived.

'The dragon's home was a cave, which was inside a hill. The entrance of the cave was surrounded by black rocks. The rocks were black because flames had come from the dragon's mouth and burned them. Many knights had tried to kill the dragon, but they had failed. Their bones lay on the ground outside the cave.

'Tristram watched the cave from the top of a hill. He saw three knights riding towards the cave. They carried swords and shields and spears.

'Then smoke and flames came from the cave. Tristram heard the cries of men and the sounds of fighting.

'Tristram got on his horse and rode towards the cave. The dragon was standing by the bodies of the dead knights. The dragon's back was covered in hard, green and blue skin. It had long, sharp claws[44] on its feet. Its teeth were sharp and white and smoke came from its mouth.

'Tristram lifted his spear and rode his horse straight towards the dragon. The dragon opened its mouth to burn the knight. Tristram's spear went into the dragon's mouth and down its throat.

'The dragon roared loudly. Then it struck its claws into the body of Tristram's horse and killed it. Tristram was thrown to the ground, but he got up quickly.

'The dragon was badly wounded. Tristram's spear was in its throat. When the dragon finally fell to the ground, Tristram ran towards it. He drove his sword into the dragon's soft stomach and killed it.'

The Knights of the Round Table were enjoying this story. They laughed and smiled.

Tristram claims Iseult for King Mark

The minstrel held up his hand and continued his story.

'Tristram cut off the dragon's head and took it to King Gurman. "You have been to this court before," said Queen Isaud. "You are a minstrel. You taught my daughter to play the harp. Are you also a knight?"

'Tristram answered in a clear voice. "Yes," he replied. He turned towards King Gurman. "I am Sir Tristram of Lyonesse," he said. "I am the Champion of King Mark of Cornwall. I have killed the dragon. Now King Mark can marry your daughter. My king no longer wants to make war against Ireland. He wants peace between our two countries."

'King Gurman turned and spoke to Queen Isaud. "Sir Tristram is a good and honest knight," he said. "The marriage between King Mark and our daughter will bring honour to both our countries."

'"Prepare my ship," said King Gurman. "Sir Tristram will take our daughter Iseult to Cornwall. There, she will marry King Mark."

'That night, Queen Isaud spoke secretly to her daughter's servant. "I have made a love potion[45]," she told him. "The potion is in this bottle of wine. You must take the bottle to Cornwall. There, King Mark and my daughter Iseult must drink the wine on their wedding day. It will make them love each other forever. Do not let anyone else drink the wine."

'Then Tristram and Iseult left Ireland. The wind was fresh. The ship sailed swiftly like a white bird. Tristram and Iseult talked and laughed in the spring sunlight. Tristram was sailing home. Soon Iseult began to fall in love with the young knight.'

The love potion

'Iseult's servant did not like the sea. She felt ill, so she lay down and slept. And while she slept, Tristram saw the bottle of wine. "Let us drink and be happy," he said to Iseult.

'Tristram and Iseult drank the love potion. Already they loved one another and the potion made their love stronger. Now they loved one another until the ending of the world, and they loved with a love greater than any in the world.

'The ship reached Cornwall and King Mark welcomed Tristram. "You are my greatest knight and my champion," said King Mark. "And Iseult is the fairest maiden in the world. We shall be married immediately."

'So, King Mark married Iseult the Fair. But Iseult loved Tristram and after her wedding to King Mark, Queen Iseult met Sir Tristram in secret. They met in forests and places where no one saw them. But people soon began to talk about Iseult the Fair and the king's champion. The other knights spoke to King Mark. "Your wife and the Champion are untrue to you. They are lovers," said the knights.'

Tristram and Iseult are parted

'When King Mark heard this news, he was angry. "If this is true, then Tristram must die," he said. "And Iseult shall live in a nunnery so that no man may see her face again."

'But King Mark was not a cruel man. He loved Iseult and remembered the brave deeds of his champion, Sir Tristram.

'King Mark spoke to Tristram: "Leave my kingdom and never return," he said. "You will never see Iseult the Fair again."'

Here, the minstrel ended his story.

No one spoke in the great hall of Camelot. There was only one sound – the sound of someone crying. Tears were falling from Lancelot's eyes.

'Minstrel, how do you know this sad story?' asked King Arthur. 'And is it a true story?'

'Yes, Sire,' answered the minstrel. 'I know that the story is true because I am Tristram of Lyonesse.'

'Welcome, Sir Tristram of Lyonesse,' said Arthur. 'There is a seat for you here at the Round Table.'

Sir Tristram becomes a Knight of the Round Table

So, Tristram stayed in Camelot and became a Knight of the Round Table. He did many good deeds and lived happily in Camelot. But he never forgot Iseult the Fair and he wanted to see her again.

Tristram married, several years later. His wife's name was also Iseult – but she was called Iseult of the White Hands. Tristram was a kind and good husband, but he did not love his wife. Sir Tristram loved Iseult the Fair. His wife, Iseult of the White Hands, knew this and she was jealous. Even after King Mark died, Tristram of Lyonesse could not be with Iseult the Fair because he was married to Iseult of the White Hands.

Tristram sends for Iseult

One day, a man attacked Tristram while he was riding in Lyonesse. Tristram fought the man and killed him. But the man had a poisoned spear which wounded Tristram in the thigh.

'I am going to die,' Tristram said to his servant, Kurwenal. 'There is poison in the wound, and it cannot heal. Only Iseult the Fair can save me. She is a great healer, like her mother. Take a ship to Tintagel and fetch the Fair Iseult.'

Then Tristram spoke to Kurwenal again. 'I may die before Fair Iseult arrives,' he said. 'Or she may not come at all. So, I beg you, make me this promise: if Iseult the Fair comes, raise a white sail on your ship. If she will not come, raise a black sail.

If I see a white sail, I will live until Fair Iseult comes to heal me.'

Iseult of the White Hands heard these words and there was jealousy in her heart as she watched Kurwenal leave for Tintagel. But she looked after her husband and did not speak of her feelings.

The black sail and the white sail

Kurwenal sailed to Tintagel and spoke to Queen Iseult the Fair. 'Sir Tristram is wounded,' he said. 'He will die unless you help him. He asks you to come with me to Lyonesse.'

So Iseult the Fair left Tintagel to help Tristram. She sailed with Kurwenal towards Lyonesse.

Kurwenal remembered his promise to Tristram. He raised a white sail on the ship.

At last, they came near to Sir Tristram's castle on the coast. Tristram was very ill. He could not rise from his bed. He was dying.

'Is Kurwenal returning? Is his ship near?' he asked his wife, Iseult of the White Hands. 'Do you see the sail? What colour is the sail?'

Iseult of the White Hands looked out of the window. She saw a ship with a white sail on the sea. But there was jealousy in her heart. 'I see a black sail,' she said.

The death of Tristram and Iseult

Then Tristram's great heart broke. 'I will never see Iseult the Fair again!' he said softly. He turned his face from the window and died.

And when Iseult the Fair came to Tristram, she found that he was dead. She knelt beside her lover and wept. But Tristram and Iseult could not be parted by death. Their love was so strong that Iseult the Fair lay down and died beside the noble Tristram.

Tristram and Iseult were buried[46] together in 'one grave[47]. Iseult of the White Hands planted two rose bushes on their grave. One bush was of red roses and the other bush was of white roses. And the two bushes grew together and became one.

9

Percivale and Lancelot

Percivale goes to Caerleon

Percivale grew up in the land west of Caerleon. It was a wild and empty land and few travellers went there. Percivale looked after his family's goats.

One day, Sir Lancelot rode through the wild land and saw Percivale. Percivale was a tall and strong young man with fair hair. He was looking after goats near the roadway.

'You are a fine young man,' said Lancelot lightly. 'You will make a good squire at the king's court. Go to Caerleon and say that Sir Lancelot sent you.'

Lancelot spoke lightly, but Percivale listened seriously. 'I will go to the king's court at Caerleon and see these knights,' Percivale told his mother. 'I do not want to look after goats all my life.'

His mother said, 'You are young and innocent. You do not know the ways of the world. Do not go to Caerleon.'

But Percivale went to Caerleon to see the king's court. He walked into the castle where the knights were feasting and he saw King Arthur.

The Red Knight

Arthur was talking to Sir Kay. He was holding a golden cup in his hand. It was the cup from which all knights drank at the Round Table.

Suddenly, a strange knight came into the hall. The knight was wearing red armour.

'Give me that cup,' said the Red Knight. 'I will drink to the best knight here.' Then he took the cup from Sir Kay's hand, left the hall and rode away.

'Who will fetch my gold cup from the Red Knight?' asked Arthur.

'I will go!' shouted all the knights at once.

'This Red Knight is unworthy[48] of a Knight of the Round Table,' Arthur said. 'Send a squire to fetch my cup.'

Then Percivale stepped forward. He was wearing the simple clothes of a goat-herd. 'I will fetch your cup,' he said.

Sir Kay laughed. 'What can a goat-herd do against a knight?'

'I want to be a knight,' said Percivale.

Sir Kay laughed again, but Arthur spoke gently. 'Young man,' he said, 'you have an honest face. If you can bring me the gold cup, I will make you a knight. Now, you may take a horse and follow the Red Knight.'

Percivale mounted a horse and rode after the Red Knight. Arthur spoke to Sir Gawain and Sir Gareth. 'Ride after him. Look after him and make sure that he comes to no harm.' And so Gawain and Gareth rode after the young Percivale.

Percivale rode quickly and soon found the Red Knight. 'That gold cup is not yours,' he called out.

The Red Knight stopped his horse and turned to Percivale. 'What can a young boy like you do against a knight?' he asked.

'I will fight you,' said Percivale, 'because you are an unworthy and untrue knight.'

'Then I will have to kill you,' said the Red Knight. He pointed his lance and rode at Percivale. But Percivale was quick. He jumped from his horse and pulled the Red Knight's spear from his hand. Then the Red Knight turned and drew his sword. But Percivale ran at the knight and drove the spear into the knight's throat. The Red Knight fell from his horse and Percivale picked up the golden cup.

57

Sir Gawain and Sir Gareth saw the cup in Percivale's hand, and they saw the dead knight on the ground. They took Percivale back to Caerleon and spoke to the king.

'This young man killed the Red Knight and took the cup,' they told him. 'He is brave enough and worthy enough to be a knight.'

So Percivale became a knight. Sir Lancelot taught Percivale to use a sword and they rode to Camelot together.

Naciens the hermit[49]

Then, at Easter time, a holy hermit called Naciens came to Camelot. 'I come to ask for help,' he said to King Arthur. 'I know a lady who is imprisoned in a tower. Only a brave and pure knight can save her. She is being kept prisoner by an evil sorceress.'

'Sire,' Lancelot said, 'I will rescue the lady. And I will take Sir Percivale with me.'

'I thank you,' said the hermit and looked at the Round Table. 'I see there is an empty seat. Who sits there?'

'No man sits in the Siege Perilous,' Arthur answered. 'Many years ago, Merlin said that only the purest, most worthy knight would one day come to sit there.'

Naciens the hermit looked at the Siege Perilous and nodded his head. Then he led Sir Lancelot and Sir Percivale out of Camelot. After a long journey, they came to a dark hillside with a black tower on the top of the hill.

'That is the Dolorous Tower,' said the hermit. 'The lady is a prisoner in that tower.'

The Dolorous Tower

So Lancelot and Percivale rode up to the tower. The door was made of wood and was fastened with an iron lock. Lancelot and Percivale struck the iron lock with their swords and the door opened.

When they broke the door, they also broke the spell that kept the lady prisoner. The lady of the tower spoke to the knights and said, 'I am the Lady Blanchefleur. I was a prisoner of Queen Morgana Le Fey. She is an enemy of my father. Now, will you come to my father so that he may thank you. My father lives in Castle Carbonek.'

King Pelles

The knights and Lady Blanchefleur rode across a waste land to an old castle. Here, two squires met them and took their horses. Then the squires led the knights into the castle hall.

An old king lay on a bed in the hall. 'I am King Pelles,' he said. 'Years ago I was wounded in the thigh. That wound will not heal. I cannot rise from this bed. I thank you for rescuing my daughter. I ask you to stay here and rest.'

The first vision[50] of the Holy Grail

So Lancelot and Percivale rested in the castle. They ate in the great hall. And while they were eating, they heard the sound of music. A bright light shone from high above. Then three women came into the hall. They were dressed in white and their faces were covered in white cloth. The first woman carried a spear. The second woman carried a dish. And the third woman carried a cup that was filled with light. The three women looked at Percivale and Lancelot. Then, the light slowly faded and the women disappeared.

Lancelot and Percivale wondered at this sight. 'What does this mean?' asked Lancelot.

'It is a vision of the Holy Grail,' King Pelles said. 'It is a vision that will come to Camelot. And when you see this

'It is a vision of the Holy Grail,' King Pelles said.

vision, the knights of Camelot will quest for the Holy Grail.'

'But why do we see the vision here and now?' asked Lancelot.

'I am the guardian[51] of this vision,' said King Pelles. 'I am descended from Joseph of Arimathea who brought the Grail to this land. You have come to this castle for a reason – though I do not know why.'

Lancelot and Percivale did not know the meaning of this vision. Percivale spent much time in prayer and wondered about the meaning of the Holy Grail. Lancelot spent much time with the Lady Blanchefleur and Blanchefleur fell in love with him.

Lancelot lies with Blanchefleur

'I must return to Camelot,' Lancelot said to Blanchefleur. But Blanchefleur was sad and did not want to let him go.

They stayed together all that day and all that night. Lancelot gave Blanchefleur a son – though he did not know of this for many years.

Lancelot and Percivale returned to Camelot and told their stories. Lancelot talked and laughed with Guinevere. But he never spoke of Blanchefleur and their secret love, and soon he forgot about her.

10

The Siege Perilous

Empty seats at the Round Table

Many years had passed. New knights had come to Camelot and old knights had died. Some knights died in quests and others died in battle. There were now empty seats at the Round Table.

Sir Bedivere and Sir Bors sat on Arthur's right. To his left sat Kay and Gareth. Opposite him sat Lancelot and Percivale and Gawain. But there was an empty seat on either side of Gawain and an empty seat beside Sir Bors.

'Who shall sit in these empty places?' asked Arthur. And he looked at the Siege Perilous which had been empty for twenty-four years. No man had ever dared to sit on the Siege Perilous because of Merlin's warning – '*He who sits on this chair will die.*'

Mordred and Galahad

At Whitsun, the holy hermit Naciens returned to Camelot. He brought a young man who was nearly sixteen years old.

Morgana Le Fey also brought a young man to Camelot. Morgana wore the clothes of a holy woman. Her head was covered so that no man could see her face.

Naciens the hermit spoke to Arthur. 'I am Naciens of Carbonek. I bring a squire to your court. I hope he will become a knight. His name is Galahad. I have raised him as my own son. I do not know his father and mother. King Pelles sent him to me when he was a few days old.'

Galahad had a fair and open face. He looked like Lancelot. But Lancelot was worldly and proud. Galahad looked more like a priest than a knight – a quiet young man with a bright and peaceful smile. Galahad was the son of Lancelot by Blanchefleur of Carbonek – though no one knew this secret.

Then the nun, whose face was hidden, stepped forward. 'I am Morgana of Glastonbury,' she said to Arthur. 'I bring a squire to your court. I hope he will become a knight. His name is Mordred.'

Mordred was short and dark and broad. He had the body of a bear and a friendly smile – a smile that masked his evil mind. Men liked him at once. They said that he reminded them of King Arthur.

Arthur had never known his father. He did not know that Mordred looked like Uther Pendragon. And he did not know that Mordred was his own son by Morgana. Also, he did not know that Morgana of Glastonbury was his own half-sister.

Morgana Le Fey brings evil to Camelot

Morgana Le Fey knew most of Merlin's secrets. She was the wisest woman in the world. But her magic had no power over Arthur. While Arthur wore the sword Excalibur, Morgana could not touch him with her magic. But Morgana still had the power to make trouble in the court.

The Knights of the Round Table stood up and welcomed Galahad and Mordred. 'We need young men,' said Bors. 'Welcome to Camelot.'

All the knights and ladies walked and talked in the hall. Then it was time for the feast. 'Be seated, knights and ladies,' said Arthur. 'And let our new squires take a seat at the Round Table. There are two empty places.'

Then Morgana worked her magic of confusion. The knights and ladies took their places, talking and laughing with joy. They paid no attention to the new squires Mordred and Galahad.

Mordred spoke to Galahad. 'There is an empty place on either side of Sir Gawain,' he said. 'Please sit on Sir Gawain's right and I will sit on his left.'

'You are very kind,' said Galahad. 'I thank you.' And Mordred smiled an evil smile.

Galahad sits on the Siege Perilous

All the knights and ladies sat down at the table. And only then did Arthur see that something was wrong. There were no empty places opposite him at the table. No man had dared to sit in the Siege Perilous for twenty-four years. But now Galahad sat in the chair and it was no longer empty.

The second vision of the Holy Grail

As Arthur saw this, there came the sound of a great bell from above the earth. Then music came, from high above, together with the sound of voices singing. The hall was filled with light and the knights and ladies looked at one another in astonishment. Then three ladies came into the hall. They were dressed in white and their faces were covered with white cloth. The first woman carried a spear. The second woman carried a dish. And the third woman carried a cup that was filled with light.

The light was so bright that the knights and ladies could not see the cup. But they were filled with joy and peace. They looked at the cup in wonder. Only Mordred hid his eyes in his hands. He could not look upon the holy cup and he wept. Mordred was unworthy.

A voice spoke softly and clearly. 'Seek the Grail. Only the purest knights can find the Grail.'

The vision faded and all the men and women in the hall were silent and astonished. They looked at King Arthur.

The quest

Arthur spoke. 'Who will seek the Grail?' he asked. 'This is the highest and holiest quest that has come to Camelot. Perhaps it will be the final quest of many knights. Seek the Grail for the honour of Logres and the Glory of God.'

11

The Quest for the Holy Grail

Bedivere and Mordred remain in Camelot

And so the Knights of the Round Table left Camelot. 'We will seek the Holy Grail, for the honour of our King and the Glory of God,' they declared.

Arthur stayed at Camelot with Bedivere and Mordred. All the other Knights of the Round Table set out to seek the Holy Grail.

Bedivere was wounded and had the use of only one hand. So Mordred offered to care for him and to serve the king at court.

Mordred soon learnt about all the rooms in the palace. He knew all the passages and gardens and hallways. He talked to the ladies of the court and heard all their gossip. He talked to the servants and learned all the secrets of the palace.

Months passed. Knights returned to Camelot with news and then set out again in search of the Holy Grail. They searched the Kingdom of Logres for news or for signs of the holy cup. Some knights never returned. They sought the Grail through dark forests and across wild hills and in deep valleys. They fought with wolves and ogres. Knights fell and were lost with no one to tell their story.

'Camelot is empty,' Mordred said to King Arthur. 'We must not lose the traditions of Camelot. We need young knights who can serve the King, the Round Table and the Kingdom of Logres. We need more young knights.'

Arthur listened to Mordred and made new knights. But the young knights quickly became loyal[52] to Mordred and not to Arthur.

Sir Bedivere was silent. He guarded King Arthur and watched and waited.

The Grail Chapel in the Wild Wood

Meanwhile, after many adventures, five knights came together in the Wild Wood near the Castle of Carbonek. Gawain and Bors met Galahad and Percivale and they were joined by Lancelot.

Naciens, the holy hermit of Carbonek, came to them out of the Wild Wood.

'The end of the quest is near. The Chapel of the Grail is hidden in the Wild Wood,' he said. 'Take King Pelles from his castle. Carry him through the wood and you will find the Grail Chapel.'

The five knights went to Castle Carbonek where King Pelles lay on his bed. 'I am in great pain,' said King Pelles. 'The wound that will not heal is painful. You must carry me to the Chapel of the Grail.'

The five knights carried King Pelles on their shields. They went into the Wild Wood and followed a narrow path. The Lady Blanchefleur walked behind them, but she did not speak to Lancelot or Galahad.

Only worthy knights may enter the Grail Chapel

Night fell. The knights walked through the Wild Wood and found their way by moonlight. There were noises in the wood and strange lights and ghostly shapes. At last the knights came to a place where the trees did not grow. A white chapel appeared in the moonlight.

'Carry me into the chapel,' said King Pelles. 'I will be healed there.'

The knights carried him to the chapel door but they could

not enter. Lancelot, Gawain and Bors pushed at the door but it did not open. Then Galahad and Percivale put their hands on the door and the door opened.

Percivale and Galahad carried the wounded king into the chapel. The Lady Blanchefleur entered the chapel with them. But Lancelot, Gawain and Bors could only watch from the doorway. They could not enter because they were not worthy or pure enough.

The third vision of the Holy Grail

The light inside the chapel grew brighter. Percivale and Galahad carried the wounded king to the altar.

Music could be heard from above. It was the music of angels singing. Then three women, dressed in white, appeared in the chapel. The first woman carried a spear. The second woman carried a dish. And the third woman carried a cup that was filled with light. They carried the spear, the dish and the cup to the altar.

Galahad went to the altar. He took the spear and handed it to Percivale. 'Heal the king's wound with this spear,' he said.

Percivale took the spear and touched it to the thigh of King Pelles. The wound was healed at last.

King Pelles sighed. 'I have been the Guardian of the Grail for many years,' he said. 'Now my wound is healed and my task is ended. I hand this task to you, Percivale. I ask you to care for the chapel and my daughter. Now I will rest.'

Then King Pelles fell into a deep sleep and did not wake again in this world. Percivale took Blanchefleur's hand and they looked at Galahad.

Galahad drinks from the Grail and passes from this world

Galahad took the Grail from the altar and raised it to his lips. He drank from the cup and the light grew brighter. The roof of the chapel opened and the light of heaven shone down. Galahad looked upwards and put his hands together in prayer. Then, as the others watched, Galahad rose up into the light.

Those who saw this sight were filled with peace and joy. Then, when the light faded and the music ended, the knights took the body of King Pelles outside. They buried the king at the door of the Grail Chapel.

The guardians of the Grail Chapel

Percivale did not return to Camelot. He married Blanchefleur and became King of Carbonek. Percivale and Blanchefleur guarded the Chapel of the Grail and some time later, they had a son called Lohengrin.

Lancelot, Gawain and Bors returned to Camelot and told their story to the court. King Arthur was filled with joy by the story of the Grail. 'This is the greatest achievement of our knights,' he said. 'This story will be told for as long as men tell stories. And while men tell this story, Camelot will never end.'

But Lancelot did not tell all the story. He did say that he could not enter the Grail Chapel. He did not say that he was unworthy. Mordred smiled an evil smile and looked at Lancelot. Lancelot turned his eyes to Guinevere.

69

12

The Breaking of the Round Table

Mordred's knights at Camelot

Many knights did not return to Camelot. They were lost in the Quest for the Holy Grail. Young knights came to Camelot and soon there was a division in the court. The old knights surrounded King Arthur. The young knights gathered around Mordred.

Mordred said to the young knights, 'King Arthur is old. Soon there will be changes in Camelot. We will have a new king and many things will be different.'

Mordred watched Lancelot and Guinevere closely. He saw them ride together and followed them when they rode into the forest. He watched while they hunted deer together. He told his friends, 'Guinevere is closer to Lancelot than to her husband King Arthur.'

Arthur had heard the rumours, but he refused to believe them. There was peace in the Kingdom of Logres. Arthur was happy to rule wisely and well. He ate and drank at the Round Table. He welcomed many knights and heard their stories, but he no longer rode out in search of adventure. His hair had turned from the colour of gold to the colour of silver.

Mordred spoke to his mother, Morgana Le Fey. 'How can we make Arthur believe that Lancelot and Guinevere are unfaithful[53] to him?' he asked.

Mordred plots against Lancelot and Guinevere

'There is a secret garden in the woods,' said Morgana Le Fey. 'Lancelot and Guinevere meet there. I will put a magic spell on the garden so that Lancelot and Guinevere fall asleep. When they are asleep, you will fetch Arthur and show him that his wife and his champion knight are lovers.'

Mordred watched and waited. He saw Lancelot and Guinevere ride out of Camelot. It was the month of May and the road was covered with white flowers. The knight and the queen rode into the wood. They came to the secret garden and sat down on the grass among the flowers. Suddenly they felt tired and soon they were asleep – lying side by side.

Lancelot and Guinevere in the secret garden

Mordred rode back to Camelot and went to the King. 'Sire,' he said, 'I saw two horses in the wood. The horses had no riders and they are the horses of Sir Lancelot and Our Lady Queen. Perhaps they have fallen or some accident has happened…'

So Arthur rode into the wood. Mordred led him to the secret garden. There Arthur saw Lancelot and Guinevere asleep on the grass among the flowers. They had their arms around each other.

As Arthur drew his sword Excalibur, Mordred smiled an evil smile. 'I will kill this false knight,' said Arthur. Then, as he raised his sword to kill Sir Lancelot, Merlin's words came into his mind.

'You will not draw the sword Excalibur in anger. You will draw that sword only to defend the right. And, while you fight for good against evil, you cannot fall in battle. The sword will protect you and you will defend the land.'

Arthur drove the sword into the ground next to Sir Lancelot's head. Then he turned away and rode back to Camelot. Mordred went with him and told everyone what had happened in the wood. Soon all the court knew that Lancelot and Guinevere had been unfaithful to their lord the King.

Lancelot and Guinevere escape from Camelot

Soon Lancelot and Guinevere awoke in the secret garden. They saw the sword Excalibur and cried out in terror. 'Arthur!' Guinevere cried. 'What shall we do? Where shall we hide?'

'Take the sword Excalibur,' said Lancelot. 'No man has ever touched it except Arthur. Take it and keep it until the King needs it for battle.'

Then Lancelot took Guinevere away into the west. 'We have sinned[54] badly,' he said. 'We have been unfaithful to our lord the King. Now we must part forever. We cannot go back to Camelot and we cannot go forward together.'

Guinevere enters a nunnery

Lancelot took Guinevere to the nunnery at Amesbury in the West Country. Guinevere carried the sword Excalibur with her for the King's great need. There the women took the queen into their nunnery and she became a nun. 'Shut me behind high walls,' she said, 'so that no man may see my sin and shame.' And so she lived in a simple room and spent her days in prayer. But she kept the sword Excalibur hidden in her room. It was her last service to her king and husband.

Lancelot becomes a hermit

Lancelot rode into the west. He left his armour and sword at a church and became a hermit. He lived alone in the woods and never spoke to anyone again.

Mordred makes war against Arthur

Meanwhile, Mordred gathered the young knights around him. 'Arthur has lost his power,' he said. 'It is time we had a new king – a young king. The Round Table is old and powerless.

We will fight the old knights and there will be a new beginning in this land.'

And so there was war in the land for the first time since the Battle of Badon Hill. Mordred and the young knights attacked Camelot. Sir Gawain and Sir Bors led the old knights out of the castle and they battled with Mordred on the banks of the river.

'Where is Arthur?' Mordred called. 'Is he afraid to fight us?'

Arthur sat in his great hall. He sat at the Round Table with his faithful knight Sir Bedivere. 'The Round Table is broken,' he said. 'We shall never see such a gathering of noble knights again.'

Gawain and Bors pushed Mordred's men back to the river. Morgana Le Fey helped her son by sending confusion among the knights. But the spell confused Mordred's men as well and Mordred had to call them back.

The death of Gawain and Bors

Bors fell on the bridge across the river. Many men died on that bridge. They fell into the river and their bodies floated to the sea.

Before he left the battlefield, Mordred rode behind Gawain who fought alone. Mordred swung his black war axe and split Gawain's helmet. Gawain fell from his horse and died in a field close to Camelot.

Mordred took his men and destroyed the lands to the west. He burned the towns and villages. He killed many men, women and children. And his army grew larger. He promised his men, 'You can keep what you can take.' And his men robbed and burned the countryside. They were like the invaders from across the sea who came before Arthur's time.

Then Morgana, his mother, spoke and said, 'Arthur has lost

the sword Excalibur. He will look for it in the West Country. I know where the sword came from. We will go to the place and wait. It is a place of power. I will be strong there. Arthur will come. We will fight him, and that will be Arthur's end.'

Arthur gathered all his men and rode after Sir Mordred. Mordred moved west and Arthur followed. Slowly they moved ever further west. Winter came and still they moved ever more slowly towards the land of the sunset.

Guinevere gives Excalibur to Arthur

Arthur came at night to the holy house at Amesbury. The nuns admitted him to Guinevere's cell. Guinevere could not speak or look at Arthur. She took the sword Excalibur from beneath her simple bed and handed it to the king.

'You are the only person to touch this sword,' said Arthur. 'Since the time I took it from the Lady of the Lake, no other person has held it. Remember me, and may we meet again in another life. Then, I pray, we shall know each other for the first time.'

And so he left the nunnery and Guinevere remained. She lived out her days as a nun and never spoke again.

Merlin comes to Arthur in his sleep

Arthur pushed Sir Mordred back to the land's end. They passed through deep forests where the sun barely shone. They came to bare hills where no man lived and nothing grew.

From these hills, Arthur saw a valley and a lake in the far west. Beyond the lake lay a plain of sand. Beyond the plain of sand lay the ocean and, far off, distant islands where the sun sets. Here, Mordred could go no further and he and Arthur prepared for their final battle.

Arthur rested that night beside the cold and misty lake. Far away, in the middle of the great wood, Merlin woke for a short time from his long sleep. And Merlin's voice came to Arthur in a dream and spoke of Excalibur and the Lady of the Lake. *'One day you must give it back to her,'* he had said. And Arthur had asked: *'How shall I know that day?'* *'You will know that day when you come to this lake again,'* Merlin had answered. *'Now, it is time for battle.'*

And Merlin came to Morgana in her sleep. 'Remember the dragon,' he said. So Morgana rose and prepared her spells to defend her son against her brother.

And Merlin also came to Lancelot in his sleep. 'Take your sword and go to your king,' he said. So Lancelot rose and took his sword from the church and rode into the west.

The last battle in the West

Arthur rose and prepared for battle. He prepared to fight Mordred on the plain of sand. Then a strange mist came over the sand. It was the last day of the old year. It was a cold day and the sun was dim. Soon the mist covered the sand and no man could see the sun.

Morgana used her magic. She called the mist from out of the lake, and she sent confusion among the knights. All day long they fought and even Arthur was confused. Men could not see each other clearly in the mist. They fought against shadows and killed friends as well as enemies.

Then the winter sunlight broke through the mist and a knight appeared. His sword shone in the gleam of sunlight. It was Lancelot. He charged at Mordred's men and drove them back towards the ocean shore. The mist cleared for a moment and Arthur's men charged forward.

Morgana saw that Lancelot was winning the battle. She spoke words of great power. It was the most powerful spell she had ever spoken. It was the spell that gave her the breath of the dragon. She breathed in the face of Arthur's men, even as Lancelot prepared to kill Mordred.

Lancelot was driven backwards by the breath of the dragon. Mordred leapt forward and swung his black war axe. Lancelot fell and died on the plain of sand. And all around him men fought on in the mist.

But the dragon spell was too powerful for Morgana. She breathed fire and it burned her. She fell to the ground and was covered with fire. All her evil burned in the fire and she died.

The death of Mordred

The mist cleared. The field was filled with dead knights. Arthur stood alone with Sir Bedivere. Bedivere could not fight because of his wounded hand. All the other Knights of the Round Table were dead. And all the enemies of Arthur were dead except for Mordred.

Mordred walked across the bloody field towards King Arthur. He carried his black war axe and Arthur held the sword Excalibur.

Arthur and Mordred fought as the sun sank low in the west. And Arthur drove his sword Excalibur into the body of Mordred and killed him. But, before he fell, Mordred swung his black war axe and struck King Arthur on the head.

13

The Passing of Arthur

Arthur returns Excalibur to the Lady of the Lake

Sir Bedivere carried King Arthur to a chapel that stood on a narrow strip of land. On one side lay the lake and on the other lay the ocean. The moon was full.

'I shall die before the morning,' said King Arthur. 'Take my sword Excalibur and throw it into the lake.'

Sir Bedivere took the sword, sadly, and walked to the lake. He looked at the sword and saw that it was beautiful. 'It is too good to throw away,' he thought. And so he hid the sword in the grass beside the lake and walked back to the wounded king.

'What did you see?' Arthur whispered.

'Nothing,' said Sir Bedivere.

'Go again and do as I told you,' said King Arthur.

Sir Bedivere went to the lake a second time and looked at the sword. 'Who will remember King Arthur when this sword is lost?' he thought. And so he hid the sword a second time.

'What did you see?' Arthur whispered. His voice was becoming weaker.

'Nothing,' said Sir Bedivere.

Then Arthur was angry. 'Does no one obey a dying king?' he asked. 'Now, on your honour, go and do what I told you. This is my last request and final command.'

Then Bedivere went quickly to the lake. He took the sword and closed his eyes and threw Excalibur into the middle of the lake. When he looked, he saw the sword flash in the moonlight and fall towards the water. But the sword did not sink into the lake. A hand rose from the water. The hand was covered in white cloth. The hand caught the sword and waved it three times. Then the Lady of the Lake pulled the sword beneath the water.

Bedivere ran back to the wounded king. Arthur looked at Bedivere's face. 'I know that you have done what I commanded,' he said. 'Now carry me to the ocean shore, but be quick. I fear that I shall die.'

Three queens carry Arthur to Avalon

Bedivere carried Arthur to the ocean shore. A boat appeared in the moonlight. It moved without wind, sails or oars. Three queens stood in the boat. It was decorated with rich red cloth. Bedivere laid Arthur on a bed of rich red cushions. The three queens wept.

'Where will you go?' Sir Bedivere asked.

Arthur answered slowly. 'I am going a long way with these women. I am going to the island valley of Avalon. It is an isle of rest where winter never comes. There I will be healed of my wound and will rest and wait. And one day I shall come again, for Merlin called me the Once and Future King.'

'And where shall I go?' asked Sir Bedivere.

'You shall travel through the world,' said Arthur. 'You shall tell of what you saw and what you heard – the stories of the Knights of the Round Table. The stories shall be told until the ending of the world.'

Then the three queens sang a sad song as the boat moved away from the shore. The boat gleamed in the moonlight.

The last of the Knights

Bedivere walked back to the cold bare hills. From the hills he looked across the water. He saw the boat. It was small but bright. The boat moved slowly towards the islands in the west.

The sword reads: *Cast me away*

'*The stories shall be told until the ending of the world.*'

The islands were lost in the darkness of night. But the boat gleamed in the last light of the frosty moon.

Bedivere watched for a long time. The moon faded. Behind him, dawn broke. Bedivere saw the last gleam of Arthur's boat in the first light of day. He heard a great shout of many voices, and then the gleam was gone.

The hills were bare but bright as Bedivere began to walk towards the east. And the sun rose on a new day.

Points For Understanding

1

1 The army of Uther attacked Tintagel Castle. What did the army of Uther do exactly?
2 How was Uther able to enter Tintagel Castle?

2

1 Who were Arthur's parents and why did he live with Sir Ector?
2 How did Arthur become King of Britain?

3

1 What was the difference between the Sword of Right and the Sword of Might?
2 How will Arthur know when to return Excalibur to the lake?

4

1 Lancelot was the Champion Knight of Camelot. Explain the meaning of the word 'champion' in the story.
2 Merlin and Nimuë spoke to each other without words. How did they speak to each other?

5

1 What did Nimuë and Morgana want from Merlin?
2 'You must rule without my help.' Why did Merlin say this to Arthur?

6

1 Why are these things important in this chapter?
  (a) an axe (b) a bargain (c) a green ribbon

7

1 What curse did the sorceress put on Sir Meliot?
2 What curse did the sorceress put on Elaine?

8

1 Explain the importance of the love potion in this story.
2 'I see a black sail,' said Iseult of the White Hands. Why did she say
  this?

9

1 Why did Sir Kay laugh at Sir Percivale?
2 What was the Holy Grail?

10

1 What was the Siege Perilous?
2 Mordred wanted Galahad to sit on the Siege Perilous. Why?
3 Why could Mordred not look at the holy cup?

11

1 Why did Mordred not go on the quest?
2 Why could Lancelot not enter the Grail Chapel?

12

1 Why did Morgana Le Fey put a spell on the secret garden in the forest?
2 Where did Arthur fight his last battle?
3 How did Morgana die?

13

1 Why did Sir Bedivere not want to cast Excalibur into the lake?
2 Where did Arthur go?

Glossary

1   **warrior** (page 4)
    an old word for a soldier.
2   **invader** – *to invade* (page 4)
    if you invade a country you take or send an army into it in order to get control of it. The people who do this are called *invaders*.
3   **empire** (page 4)
    a number of countries that are ruled by one person or government.
4   **attacked** – *to attack* (page 4)
    to use violence against a person or place.
5   **court** (page 5)
    the place where a king or queen lives and works. Someone who has an official position at the *court* of a king or queen, or who spends time there, is a *courtier*.
6   **magician** (page 5)
    someone who uses magic to make impossible things happen. A man in stories who has magic powers is also called a *wizard*. A woman who uses evil spirits to do magic in stories is called a *sorceress*.
7   **chivalrous** (page 5)
    polite and kind behaviour by men towards women.
8   **honour, truth and justice** (page 5)
    These were the things that the knights believed in. *Honour* is the respect that people have for someone who achieves something great, is very powerful, or behaves in a way that is morally right. *Truth* is the quality of being true, and someone who says what is true and does not lie *speaks truthfully*. *Justice* is treatment of people that is fair and morally right, and someone who is fair and morally right is *just*.
9   **quest** (page 5)
    a long difficult search
10 **raven** (page 9)
    a large bird with shiny black feathers.
11 **blow** (page 9)
    a hard hit from someone's hand or an object. If you *strike someone*, you hit someone or something with your hand, a tool, or a weapon. You can also say *strike (someone) a blow*. A hit made with someone's hand, a stick, or another object is also called a *stroke*.

12 **swan** (page 9)
a large white bird with a long neck that lives near water.
13 **Sire** (page 10)
an old word used for talking to a king. There are a lot of words used before people's names in this book. *Sir* is used before the name of a man who is a knight. *Lord* is used before the name of a man who has a high rank in the highest British social class. *Lady* is used as a title for some women who have important social or official positions.
14 **protect** (page 11)
to keep someone or something safe.
15 **spell** (page 11)
words or actions that are believed to make magic things happen. If you *cast a spell*, you use magic to make something happen to someone, or to seem to do this. If you *break a spell*, you end it. *Spells* can make good or bad things happen. If you *curse* someone, you use magic powers to make bad things happen to someone. These bad things are called a *curse*.
16 **wound** (page 12)
an injury in which your skin or flesh is seriously damaged. Someone who is seriously injured is *wounded*.
17 **gave birth** – *to give birth (to someone)* (page 13)
to produce a baby from inside your body. A baby that is recently born is *newborn*.
18 **nunnery** (page 13)
a place where religious women – or *nuns* – live together.
19 **archbishop** (page 14)
a priest of the highest rank in some Christian churches.
20 **astonished** (page 16)
very surprised.
21 **sign** (page 19)
a piece of evidence that something exists or is happening.
22 **plenty** (page 21)
a situation in which large supplies of something are available, especially food.
23 **deed** (page 22)
a literary word meaning something that someone does.
24 **ogre** (page 23)
a cruel frightening person.

25 **heir** (page 23)

someone who will receive money, property, or a title when another person dies.

26 **squire** (page 25)

a young man in the Middle Ages who worked for a knight and carried his shield. Squires wanted to become knights.

27 *sorceress* (page 26)

a woman who uses evil spirits to do magic in stories.

28 **half-sister** (page 27)

a sister who has either the same mother or the same father as you have.

29 **abbey** (page 28)

a large church with buildings connected to it for monks or nuns to live in. An *abbess* is a woman who is in charge of a convent (a religious community of women).

30 **Joseph of Arimathea** (page 28)

in the Christian bible, a rich man who was a supporter of Jesus.

31 **heal** (page 28)

if an injury heals, or if someone heals it, the skin or bone grows back together and becomes healthy again. Someone who can cure people who are ill, using special powers that other people do not understand, is called a *healer*.

32 **joust** (page 29)

a competition between two people riding horses. They fight by riding towards each other and trying to hit each other with a long stick called a *lance*.

33 **noble** (page 32)

behaving in a brave and honest way that other people admire.

34 **challenge** (page 33)

if you *challenge* someone, you invite them to compete or fight. This invitation is called a *challenge*.

35 **bargain** (page 35)

an agreement in which each person or group promises something.

36 **maiden** (page 37)

an old word meaning a girl or young woman who is not married. *Maid* has the same meaning.

37 **ribbon** (page 37)

a long narrow piece of coloured cloth or paper that is used for decorating or tying things.

38 **companion** (page 43)
someone who is with you or who you spend a lot of time with.
39 **tapestry** (page 44)
a thick heavy cloth that has pictures or patterns woven into it.
40 **minstrel** (page 46)
a singer or musician who travelled and performed at the time of
King Arthur.
41 **harp** (page 46)
a musical instrument that consists of a row of strings stretched over
a large upright frame.
42 **pirate** (page 48)
someone who steals things from ships while they are sailing.
43 **dragon** (page 49)
in stories, an imaginary large animal that breathes out fire.
44 **claws** (page 50)
one of the sharp curved nails that some birds and animals have on
their feet.
45 **potion** (page 51)
a drink that is believed to be magic, poisonous, or useful as a
medicine. A *love potion* is believed to make the person who drinks it
fall in love.
46 **buried** – *to bury* (page 55)
to put something in the ground and cover it with earth.
47 **grave** (page 55)
the place where a dead person is buried in a deep hole under the
ground.
48 **unworthy** (page 57)
a *worthy* person has qualities that make people respect them. An
unworthy person lacks these qualities.
49 **hermit** (page 58)
someone who chooses to live alone, or someone who spends most of
their time alone.
50 **vision** (page 59)
something that someone sees in a dream or as a religious experience.
51 **guardian** (page 61)
a person who protects something.
52 **loyal** (page 66)
someone who is loyal continues to support a person or organisation.

87

53 **unfaithful** (page 70)
   having a sexual relationship with someone who is not your
   husband, wife or usual partner.
54 **sin** – *to sin* (page 72)
   if you *sin*, you do something that is wrong according to religious
   laws. You commit a *sin*.

Exercises

Vocabulary: words in the story

Choose the best word in the following sentences.

> **Example:** The servant put ~~sugar~~ / ~~water~~ / poison / ~~spice~~ into Uther's wine. Uther drank the wine and died.

1 His eyes were the colour of the clear blue <u>sea / sky / pond / shore.</u>

2 'Winter is coming and my men have little <u>feet / mouth / sword / food</u>.'

3 Uther <u>promised / ordered / told / remembered</u> to give the child, Arthur, to Merlin.

4 'We will have a <u>feast / contest / battle / prayer</u> to see who can pull the sword from the stone.'

5 The people <u>attacked / invaded / played / suffered</u> because there was no order in the land.

6 'Father, put your sword back in its <u>box / sheath / container / holder</u>,' Arthur said.

7 The sword from the stone is a <u>sign / warning / notice / word</u> that you are king.

8 Arthur fought six battles and <u>won / lost / defeated / invaded</u> his enemies.

9 It was a time of peace and <u>plenty / party / poetry / pretty</u> and the people were happy.

10 'The empty seat is called the <u>Chair / Stool / Siege / Bench</u> Perilous,' said Merlin.

11 You may strike the first <u>go / axe / sword / blow</u> and I will strike the second.

12 'Gawain has made a terrible <u>bargain / break / choice / permit</u>,' thought the Knights.

13 It is Christmas – a time of peace and <u>party / luck / celebration / feast</u>.

14 'I <u>look / search / quest / seek</u> the Green Chapel and the Green Knight,' said Gawain.

15 'It is a cold night. Would you like a <u>maiden / ribbon / guest / squire</u> of the castle to visit you?'

16 'I have a gift for you – a piece of green ribbon. The ribbon will <u>protect / warm / thank / present</u> you.'

17 Sir Gawain did not <u>keep / make / break / take</u> his promise to the Green Knight.

18 'I have cursed Sir Meliot. Now his wound will never <u>better / heal / bleed / mark</u>.'

19 No man has gone into the Chapel Perilous and returned <u>at once / in time / arrive / alive</u>.

20 'If Iseult the Fair comes, raise a white <u>flag / sign / sail / sheet</u> on your ship.'

21 Mordred could not look at the holy cup because he was <u>ugly / blind / short / unworthy</u>.

22 The words on the sword were TAKE ME UP and <u>throw / pull / draw / cast</u> ME AWAY.

Writing: rewrite sentences

Use words from the box to rewrite these sentences. You may need to
make some changes, such as verb tenses. There are two extra words.

> ~~army~~   wounds   food   hermit   Champion   swords and axes
> companion   drive   messengers   raise   gift   battle   squire
> deeds   potion   nunnery   goat-herd   guardian   fall   protect
> white   quest

> **Example:**   *Uther was a strong king with <u>a lot of soldiers</u>.*
> You write: *Uther was a strong king with a large army.*

1 Merlin's hair was <u>the colour of snow</u>.

   Merlin's hair

2 Winter is coming and my men have <u>few supplies</u>.

   Winter is coming

3 'I will <u>keep you safe</u>,' said Merlin.

   I will

4 The armies of Uther and Gorloïs fought with <u>weapons</u>.

   The armies of

5 His body was covered in blood from many <u>cuts</u>.

   His body was

6 'I will send <u>people with messages</u> through all the lands of Britain.'

   I will send

7 He <u>lifted</u> the sword above his head and the metal flashed brightly in
   the sunlight.

   He

8 Excalibur is a <u>present</u> from the Lady of the Lake.

   Excalibur is a

9 You will fight many <u>fights between armies</u>.

   You will

10 The knights of Camelot did many great and good <u>actions</u>.

The knights

11 Two <u>young men who were going to be knights</u> held the knights' horses.

Two

12 Uther put Morgana into <u>a place where holy women live</u>.

Uther put Morgana

13 Tristram and Iseult drank the love <u>drink</u>.

Tristram and Iseult

14 Lancelot was the <u>First Knight</u> of Camelot.

Lancelot was

15 Percivale <u>looked after his family's goats</u>.

Percivale

16 The knights of Camelot will <u>go and look for</u> the Holy Grail.

The knights

17 'I am the <u>person who looks after</u> the Grail,' said King Pelles.

I am the

18 Bors <u>was killed in battle</u> on the bridge across the river.

Bors

19 Arthur <u>pushed his sword hard</u> into the body of Mordred.

Arthur

Grammar: comparisons with as ... as ...

Use the words in the box. Look at the example. Can you make similar comparisons?

~~snow~~   death   grass   sky   night   bear   blood   sun   stone

Example: *Merlin's hair was white.*
You write: *Merlin's hair was as white as snow.*

1 Uther Pendragon was strong.
_____

2 The strange knight's beard was green.
_____

3 Arthur's eyes were blue.
_____

4 Lancelot's rose was red.
_____

5 The ice on the hills was hard.
_____

6 The smoke was black.
_____

7 The light was bright.
_____

8 Sir Meliot was pale.
_____
_____

Grammar & Vocabulary: just

The knights of Camelot fight for truth, honour and *justice*. King Arthur is a noble and *just* king. But you will often hear the word JUST in spoken English with a different meaning.

NOUN JUSTICE	ADJECTIVE of justice JUST	ADVERB JUST
treatment of people that is fair and right	good and fair	1. a short time ago 2. only, simply

Is the word JUST used as an adjective or an adverb in the following sentences?

	ADJ	ADV
1 Bedivere was a just and honest man.		
2 Lancelot arrived just in time during the battle.		
3 There were just a few knights left in Camelot during the quest.		
4 Uther Pendragon was not a just and honourable king.		

Can you use the adverb JUST in the following sentences? Look at the examples.

> **Example 1:**   *We have now finished. (We finished a minute ago.)*
> You write: *We've just finished.*

> **Example 2:**   *It only takes a few minutes.*
> You write: *It takes just a few minutes. / It just takes a few minutes.*

5 You simply press the button marked SEND.

_____

6 There are three buttons, but you only press the button marked SEND.

_____

_____

_____

7 It will be ready in a very short time.

_____

8 I was only wondering if you'd like to go.

_____

9 I found you barely in time.

_____

Vocabulary choice: words which are related in meaning

Which word is most closely related? Look at the example then try to match the rest.

Example:	sword	speech	<u>weapon</u>	swear	armour
1	**gold**	ancient	colour	bear	jewel
2	**besiege**	surround	defend	attend	descend
3	**spell**	time	place	wisdom	magic
4	**poison**	medicine	healthy	murder	fish
5	**cathedral**	castle	palace	church	minstrel
6	**astonished**	amazed	bored	successful	founded
7	**might**	worth	weakness	volume	power
8	**deeds**	laws	arms	exercises	actions
9	**perilous**	safe	possible	dangerous	attractive
10	**stroke**	hit	fire	meat	boat
11	**quest**	answer	search	host	reply
12	**celebration**	festival	decoration	occasional	assembly
13	**ribbon**	band	clothing	metal	wood
14	**curse**	speak evil	speak well	say prayers	talk badly
15	**maid**	done	girl	cook	taken

Published by Macmillan Heinemann ELT
Between Towns Road, Oxford OX4 3PP
A division of Macmillan Publishers Limited
Companies and representatives throughout the world
Heinemann is the registered trademark of Pearson Education, used under licence.

ISBN 978–0–230–03444–0
ISBN 978–0–230–02685–8 (with CD pack)

This version of *King Arthur and the Knights of The Round Table* was
retold by Stephen Colbourn for Macmillan Readers

First published 2008
Text © Macmillan Publishers Limited 2008
Design and illustration © Macmillan Publishers Limited 2008
This version first published 2008

Illustrated by Janos Jantner and Martin Sanders
Cover image by Getty Images/Look

Printed and bound in Thailand

2013 2012 2011
6   5   4   3

with CD pack
2013 2012 2011
8   7   6   5